AN INTRODUCTION
TO THE BAPTISTS

BY
ERROLL
HULSE

D1188691

Carey Publications Ltd.,
5, Fairford Close,
Haywards Heath,
Sussex RH16 3EF

I am the true vine

John 15 v1

© Carey Publications Ltd.

ISBN 085479 7807

First printed 1973
Second edition, completely revised 1976

Printed by
Stanley L. Hunt (Printers) Ltd.
Midland Road, Rushden, Northants, England
for
Carey Publications Ltd.
5 Fairford Close, Haywards Heath
Sussex RH16 3EF

CONTENTS

ILLUSTRATIONS[1]

[1] Gratitude is expressed to *The Evangelical Library*, London, for the illustrations which appear on pages 32, 50, 59 and 72.

INTRODUCTION

WHO are the Baptists, and what do they believe? Where are they to be found? What is their history? Who among them have been outstanding, whether in their own circles or in the wider field? Questions such as these are dealt with in the pages which follow. The beliefs and practices of the Baptists are discussed. Historical and biographical material will include some account of Bunyan, Spurgeon and other well known Baptists of former days. The true Church still thrills with the story of what God wrought through the ministries of such men.

The New Testament story opens with the ministry of a man known pre-eminently as "the Baptist", or as Luke once calls him, "John Baptist". The subsequent ministries of the Lord Jesus Christ himself and his apostles were Baptist in the same sense, although John's baptism and theirs differed somewhat in their significance, and the former did not suffice for the latter (Acts 19: 1-5). Obviously, therefore, Baptist history has deep and ancient roots. For long years, however, Baptists as such were driven "underground"; the Church became corrupted; then came the glorious Protestant Reformation, and at that period Baptists re-emerged and bore a fresh testimony to the grace and power of God, and to the scriptural character of their faith. Their enemies were constrained to bear witness to their constancy in suffering.[1]

Origins

Various theories of Baptist origins have been held. Among these is found the idea of a succession of ministry from apostolic times to the present day, a theory akin to that of "apostolic succession" and based upon an

---

[1] Cardinal Hosius, who presided over certain sessions of the Roman Catholic Council of Trent (1546-63) had this to say of them: "If the truth of religion were to be judged of by the readiness and cheerfulness which a man of any sect shows in suffering, then the opinions and persuasions of no sect can be surer than those of the Baptists, since there have been none for these twelve hundred years past that have been more grievously punished, or that have more cheerfully undergone, and even offered themselves to, the most cruel sorts of punishments, than these people."

unprovable chain of ordination. A second concept is that of a chain of baptisms carried on by men immersed as believers. Thirdly there is the idea of church succession, based upon historical evidence for a long series of local churches bearing the true scriptural marks. Fourthly there is the concept of the succession of principles exemplified in individuals or groups who have held to the essentials of Baptist witness.

Surely it is the succession of truth that matters supremely. The standing of a church today does not depend upon ecclesiastical pedigree or historical lineage. The only sure touchstone is adherence to the doctrines of Holy Scripture. Luther claimed that "justification by faith" was basic in the proving of a church's standing or falling. This claim we also hold. Sound doctrine is fundamental; its practice is equally so. Where the two hold good, at least for long periods of time, it is a further matter for thankfulness. We do rejoice when we find an unbroken succession of Baptist Churches. The American historian, Henry C. Vedder, in his *Short History of the Baptists*, vouches for such a succession in England, as "established by indubitable documentary evidence", from about the year 1610. He further asserts that "from about the year 1641, at the latest, Baptist doctrine and practice have been the same in all essential features that they are today". This conclusion is the more satisfactory because it does not necessitate the straining of historical accuracy involved in the attempt to prove a definite continuity between earlier Baptist sectarians and modern Baptists. Such attempts have been further weakened by their stress upon comparatively superficial resemblances and the ignoring of major doctrinal differences.[1]

The watershed

After the apostolic era the Reformation forms the most important epoch in Christian history. How do the Baptists figure at this time? The problem is posed and answered as to why Luther, Calvin and Zwingli did not embrace the doctrine of believers' baptism. Further, a description is given of such stalwarts as Hubmaier, a Swiss martyr, who attempted to establish the doctrine of believers' baptism and to spread the concept of the gathered church. It was in England that Baptists of the modern age began the work of assimilating Reformation doctrine in so far as it accorded with the Word of God, while rejecting elements in that doctrine which were essentially hang-overs from the corrupt medieval period. Leaders of robust theological calibre began to pastor Baptist congregations and these congregations in their turn became nurseries of similar men.

In the Second Chapter are to be found cameos of some of these early leaders. Their contributions to the English "religious scene" were sometimes breath-taking in their scope and originality. This chapter could well be entitled "Baptist heirs of the Reformation". Early champions

---

[1] For instance Peter de Bruys rejected the Roman mass but also rejected large parts of Scripture and embraced the false doctrine of "soul-sleep".

such as Kiffin and Keach set the Baptists on a solid Reformed foundation of faith. Later Spurgeon popularised the Puritans, the second "generation" of Reformers, and their writings, probably more than any other preacher in history. It is interesting to note that while fervent attempts were made to establish the Baptist cause on the Continent, it was in fact in Britain that a solid doctrinal foundation was laid. English Baptist history, therefore, precedes other streams which flow from this source.

It was in North America, however, that the Baptists like the children of Israel in Egypt were to multiply rapidly. They became the most numerous and influential evangelical denomination. Chapter Three of our story outlines this development. It merits the closest attention. But unhappily and, in this respect, unlike the Israelites in Egypt, the Baptists have in the course of years come to suffer from another form of bondage, and the same chapter concludes with an examination of the matter.

Russia

It is unthinkable to omit reference to the witness of Baptists in Russia. Today their faith and fortitude are spoken of throughout the whole world, and well they deserve to be. They have persevered through the most bitter and persistent persecution, surviving conditions most hostile to their faith. In former generations Russian Nonconformity has been mostly of the Baptist persuasion. Baptists suffered greatly from time to time under Russian Czardom. History has repeated itself in the Communist persecution of the present century. Since 1962, over 500 Baptists have been imprisoned, although this number may, in actual fact, be very much higher since only a limited amount of information comes to the West. The sufferings and trials of believers in Russia are documented by Michael Bourdeaux in *Faith on Trial in Russia.* In other Communist countries also, Baptists are standing valiantly for the truth; at the moment such countries represent "the high places of the field" in which believers are prepared to lay down their lives for the faith.

The world picture

With regard to numbers, the Baptist World Alliance has published the statement that in 1975 there were 33,800,000 adherents throughout the world. Over 29,600,000 of these are in North America. India has 760,000, Zaire 246,000, Brazil 442,000, Burma 308,000, The U.K. 253,000, and Rumania 160,000. The figures for Russia are discussed in the chapter on Russia. An interesting story lies behind the development of the Baptist movement in each of these countries. Equally remarkable narratives could be provided for other countries where Baptists are less numerous. For instance, the way in which Johann Oncken was enabled to pioneer a movement in Germany is fascinating. His initiative was also felt in Denmark, where he was instrumental in establishing the first Baptist Church in 1839. Oncken also played a part in the establishment of the first Swedish Baptist Church which was formed in Gothenburg in 1848. His ministry in the realm of church planting was a powerful influence in other countries such as Switzerland, Holland and Russia.

This German pioneer was well-grounded in the truth and many of the newly-planted churches followed the example of the church led by Oncken at Hamburg in having a comprehensive statement of doctrinal belief including clarity on the subject of salvation by sovereign grace.

Brought up in the Lutheran church in his native town of Varel, Oncken left home in 1813, in his fourteenth year, going to stay in Scotland with a Scottish merchant whom his father knew. He was introduced to the Bible and influenced by the Presbyterians. Later he moved to London where he was converted. For nine years Oncken followed a career in merchant business, after which he settled down in Hamburg where the exercise of an active and powerful witness led to the formation of an assembly in 1834. This church declared itself distinctively Baptist, Oncken, his wife and others being immersed. At the same time Oncken was formally ordained as elder and preacher.

By 1865 the membership of the church was 719. Today the Baptists in both East and West Germany are in decline and need desperately to return to the doctrines believed and the zeal displayed by their first leader. There are now about 70,000 Baptists in West Germany and 22,000 in East Germany.

The faith of Baptists and the way ahead

An introduction to the Baptists would not be complete without reference to what they believe. It needs to be strongly asserted that unless the Baptists return to an unfeigned belief in Scripture, and to the robust theology of their forbears, they will inevitably decline in quality, in numbers and in influence. Their fine gold has become dim. If liberalism enters by one door and orthodox faith in Scripture is driven out at another, then the outlook is bleak indeed. If the practice that accompanies soundness of doctrine gives place to the worldliness which is always introduced with liberalism, Baptist churches may as well close their doors. The doctrinal indifference, feeble practice and moral permissiveness of the present age must be arrested. Only God can do this and send times of extensive reformation and revival. Certainly such outpourings would be "times of refreshing from the presence of the Lord". May he grant them! The author is well aware that some will criticise a work of this kind on the ground of its simplicity and elementary character. In anticipation of such censure, it must be pointed out that the approach is mainly pastoral. We need books for the members of our churches who are unacquainted with our history. Most of those who belong to the Baptist family today are unable to claim more than the barest smattering of knowledge of Baptist history, and the vast majority are probably ignorant of most of the names mentioned in our pages. Few popular books are available, and we plead the value of short biographical sketches in which past worthies are introduced. Valuable information is often confined to scholarly treatises which have no regard to the slight academic attainments of many readers, and which stand apart from the actual spiritual state and needs of local churches. It is as if a pulpit preacher announced that only those possessed of University qualifications would be at all competent to benefit from his discourse. On the contrary, we account it our calling that ordinary folk should hear us gladly.

Acknowledgements

The goodness of the Lord in graciously providing the means necessary for producing a book of this kind is observed with deep thankfulness by the author. Chief among these blessings is a united and affectionate church at Cuckfield whereby husband, wife and family are sustained and strengthened. Much appreciated help has been given by others, particularly Mr. S. M. Houghton of Charlbury.

Menno Simons

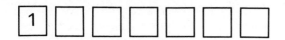

THE REFORMATION
AND BAPTISTS

After Pentecost the Reformation must surely be regarded as the most momentous event in the history of the Church of Christ. Truth sprang out of the earth and that righteousness which is imputed to those who believe in the Son of God came down in abundance from heaven. To scrutinise the lives and actions of the individual Reformers is to put one's finger on the very watershed of contemporary evangelical religion. Before the Reformation there were isolated springs of water, but they were constricted. The Reformation opened channels so that there were rivers in which to swim.

Where do the Baptists fit in? Menno Simons, probably the most successful of the early Baptists, gathered together the pieces of a battered cause and shaped an evangelical movement of considerable worth. Mennonite churches can be found to this day in countries like the United States and France. Menno Simons, however, like John Wesley after him, did not embrace the doctrine of the bondage of the will (and consequently the doctrines of grace), which was thundered out by Luther as "the hinge upon which all turns". Free Grace Baptists were to emerge later, particularly in England. The theology of the Reformation in respect of the doctrines of grace blended perfectly well with the Baptist doctrine of the church and eminent men such as Abraham Booth were to demonstrate this later in their written works.

In more recent years the Baptists were to find their David in Spurgeon. His departure from the scene midst clouds of war dust caused by the downgrade controversy was followed by serious decline in regard to the cause of Free Grace among Baptists. When it seemed that that cause could hardly become more wretched, renewed interest was rekindled through a revival of Free Grace literature during the past decade. This stirring has been largely among young men in the ministry—most of them Baptists. For them their relationship to the Reformation is more than interesting. It is crucial. Should they retain the paedobaptist doctrine of the Reformers? Why did the Reformers retain infant baptism? Did

11

*they take over Popish practice and later accommodate it in modified form
in the house of covenant theology? Did they give the subject open-minded
treatment? The Anabaptists were groping their way and were hardly in a
position to offer clearly formulated or well-reasoned arguments.
Hubmaier, in particular, was exceptional and came near to presenting a
systematic biblical case of which we would not be ashamed.*

*It can be seen then that the story of the relationship of the Reformers to
this subject is vital if we are to understand the history of ensuing centuries.
How did the leading Reformers regard the subject of baptism? Were
there any to plead with them concerning this matter? If so, who were
they and what became of them? What conclusions ought we to draw from
this history?*

WHAT happened when Luther nailed his 95 Theses to the door of the
Castle Church at Wittenberg on October 31, 1517, has been likened
to a shattering blow directed upon a large earthenware vessel. The vessel,
already riddled with cracks, immediately disintegrates into a pile of pieces.
It is a mistake to view the Reformation apart from the history preceding
it. Indeed, to understand the major issues of the Reformation one has
to grasp the nature of Constantinianism. From the time of Constantine
one can discern the tensions experienced by true believers who were
unhappy with the sacral idea, which is that the whole of society should
form a monolithic church.

The Reformation occasioned a tremendous upsurge of radical opinion in
regard to this question of the church. The radical reformers believed not
that the church should be reformed merely, but rather that the apostolic
church should be restored. In other words they believed that the Church
of Rome was beyond reformation and also that a Protestant Church along
"comprehensive" lines was inadequate.

"The Radical Reformation," as G. H. Williams described it, "was a
massive movement at the core of Christendom which embraced innumerable
people from differing backgrounds from one end of Europe to the other."
It is almost impossible to do justice to the movement because of its
tremendous diversity of character. In recent years historians have come
to recognise that a true understanding of the Reformation is impossible
without due consideration of this left wing. Moreover, an increasing
volume of research material is being made available and this has cast a
great deal of new light on the true nature of the Anabaptist movement.
Traditional interpretations have had to be changed considerably. The
entire Anabaptist movement was blackened by the excesses of the minority.
The catastrophe at Munster in 1535, particularly, has served to dub the
Anabaptist cause as fanatical and unworthy of serious attention.

Henry Bullinger, successor to Zwingli, at Zurich, wrote extensively on the Anabaptist movement, which he described as "Satanic". Bullinger became recognised as *the* authority on the subject. Fearfully biased, his work served to prejudice generations against serious consideration of the Anabaptist cause. Modern research has shown the inadequacy of Bullinger's work, and successive layers of misrepresentation are being removed. Of the modern writers, Leonard Verduin is probably the best known, because of his book *The Reformers and their Stepchildren.*[1] He describes the Anabaptist movement as "the Second Front" and chooses to tell the story using as chapter headings, the nasty names ascribed to the Anabaptists. The strength of Verduin's book is that it shows that the Anabaptists were essentially at loggerheads with the sacralism of the magisterial[2] reformers. This sacralism was maintained by equating paedobaptism with circumcision. Very simply Verduin defines sacralism as, "society held together by a religion to which all the members of that society are committed". Another strength of Verduin's book is that it illustrates that the Anabaptist thought had its roots in the preceding centuries. On the other hand the book fails to give a composite, overall and accurate picture of the movement as a whole. This is provided by G. H. Williams in his monumental study *The Radical Reformation,*[3] a volume ill-suited by reason of its size and detail for any but the most avid readers. It provides a voluminous storehouse of extremely well-documented material from which one soon learns that the left-wing movement can be likened to one of those large patchwork blankets our grandmothers used to knit—copious and very diverse in character.

To estimate what percentage of those involved in the Radical Reformation were evangelical in the sense that we understand that term today, is impossible but then this is equally true of the Protestant Church of the Reformation. We know that by 1586 the Anabaptists formed a quarter of the total population of Friesland. In many cities churches of the Radical Reformation numbered hundreds of members. In Groningen there were 1,100.[4] The amazing rapidity with which the Anabaptists spread is ascribed to the emphasis which they placed on the Great Commission. The instances that have just been cited apply to areas where the Anabaptists were not exterminated. Those who study the Radical Reformation for the first time should be warned against disillusionment in regard to some of the Reformers. Their part in the persecution of the Anabaptists is not a pleasant subject. The attention given to the long-

---

[1] Paternoster Press, 296 pp. At present out of print. Referred to as *Verduin* hereafter.

[2] They are called "Magisterial" because of their reliance on civil magistrates to maintain the cause of religion.

[3] Weidenfeld and Nicolson, 924 pp. Hereafter referred to as *Williams*.

[4] Johannes Warns in his book on baptism, Paternoster, now out of print, provides many details of this kind.

neglected left wing inevitably means the rewriting of the Reformation in some of its aspects, and the reflection on the Reformers is not always sweet, to say the least. David Marshall, in reviewing Verduin's book in the *Banner of Truth* magazine,[1] records understandable alarm. "This is hardly the time to denigrate the Reformers," he says, "when most evangelicals are tragically ignorant of the immense debt we owe to them." We fully sympathise with these sentiments. On the other hand we do not wish to live with a romanticised idea of the Reformation, or, for that matter, foster dreamland concepts of any epoch of history. When one has received incalculable blessing from the lives and teachings of the Reformers it is painful to read of their intolerance and harshness. The eminent historian Bainton confesses: "I felt intense resentment against Luther because he spoke so magnificently for liberty in the early 1520s and condoned the death penalty for the Anabaptists a decade later. Having worked for eight years on a biography of Luther in the 1940s anger changed to sadness through the discovery that in this case, as often elsewhere, it is the saints who burn the saints."[2]

Lest we be righteous overmuch about the maltreatment of the Stepchildren let us remember that the Reformers truly believed that social anarchy would prevail if the radical movement was allowed to hold sway. As far as they were concerned, the preservation of the Reformation was at stake and the church-state relationship was essential to the Reformation. Hence they sought to preserve the church-state relationship at all costs. Because of what the Lord did through them in raising up truth in the earth, the sixteenth century Reformers tower above most.

What then do we, who embrace the soteriology or the main doctrines of the Reformers, stand to learn from the Anabaptists? The answer should emerge when we see how Luther, Zwingli and Calvin reacted as they came into contact with those who rejected the doctrine of paedobaptism.

Luther

Late in December 1521, a small group of radical prophets arrived from Zwickau at Wittenberg. The leaders of this group were Storch, Stubner and Müntzer, the latter of ill-fame because of his extremely unbalanced notions—such as the claim of prophecy, the ability of inspired speech, similar to the claims of neo-Pentecostals today. Included in their attack on unscriptural practices was the rejection of infant baptism. Luther was

---

[1] *Re-writing the Reformation*, Issue 45, 1966, p. 7.

[2] Quoted from *Studies in the Reformation*, 1964.
We would not concur with Bainton's categorical statement that "saints burned saints," but rather see the secular arm of the State mixed up in all this. Just as in our day the Ecumenical Movement is mostly secular, nominally Christian, and political (even to the point of providing funds for the promotion of violence), so in the 16th century persecution of the real saints had its spring in sacralism. That genuine Christians should be implicated is sad and seems inexcusable, but who among us could say that he is without sin?

away at the Wartburg at the time and the men at Wittenberg were caught off-guard. Melanchthon, although repelled by their rejection of infant baptism, was impressed by the biblical knowledge and the cogent reasoning of the men from Zwickau. University trained, Stubner was particularly impressive. He succeeded in winning Luther's disciples, Cellarius and Westerberg, to the Anabaptist cause. Westerberg was later to become a leading Anabaptist. Carlstadt, a well-known personality in the town, was much influenced by the visitors. Eventually he came to the position where he refused to administer infant baptism. In 1524 he was banished from Electoral Saxony. Moved by the visitors the unstable Carlstadt was responsible for much unhealthy extremism.

The disturbances at Wittenberg required stern, corrective measures by Luther on his return during March 1522. The unrest created by the prophets from Zwickau and their influence upon Carlstadt particularly, did little to endear Luther to the Anabaptist movement.[1] To Luther, Müntzer became "the arch-devil", and there can be little doubt that those opposing infant baptism tended to be associated in his mind with fanatics of this kind. It is on record that Storch and Stubner of Zwickau had separate conversations with Luther on infant baptism, which induced him to write defending the view that a kind of faith is infused into infants.

Luther hardened more and more in his attitude toward the left wing. By March 1530 he gave his consent to the death penalty for Anabaptists. This was further confirmed in 1536, when he signed a document clearly stating that the Anabaptists were to be put to death, not because they were given to physical violence, but because their programme entailed a complete re-orientation of church, state and society. We can see the contrast of these later views with those held by Luther in 1520 when he wrote his *Babylonish Captivity of the Church*. In this work he considered the idea of reshaping the church as a body of believers only. We see then, in broad outline, why Luther moved further away from the Baptist concept of the church.[2]

Zwingli and the Swiss Anabaptists

A group of men very different from the Zwickau prophets, was destined to represent the Baptist cause at Zurich. To start with, we find in Zwingli a man who, at the beginning of his Reformation pilgrimage, entertained grave doubts about infant baptism. "Nothing grieves me more than that at present I have to baptise children, for I know it ought not to be done," he said. Verduin declares of Zwingli, "Here was a man who was deeply

---

[1] *Luther and his Times.* E. G. Schwiebert. Concordia, pp. 535-550.

[2] For my own part I would rather have a good biography of Luther than any other figure in church history. Following him it could be wished that there were complete and ideal biographies of William Tyndale, Spurgeon, Carey, Wycliffe, Calvin, Edwards, Knox, Bunyan, Judson and John Dod (1558-1645), the latter because we need to see the Puritan period as a whole through the eyes of one who had intimate knowledge of the scene over a long period.

aware that the renewal of the church called for a radical break with 'christening'." The matter weighed heavily with the Swiss reformer. He knew well that the civil leaders were sacralists and that they barred the way to any change in regard to infant baptism. Zwingli wrote, "I leave baptism untouched, I call it neither right nor wrong; if we were to baptise as Christ instituted it, then we would not baptise any person until he reached the age of discretion; for I find it nowhere written that infant baptism is to be practised. . . ." He added, "However we must practise infant baptism so as not to offend our fellow men".[1] To his associates he confessed, "If we were to baptise in accord with the command of Christ, then we would not baptise anyone until he has reached the age of discretion."

Zwingli's friends were well acquainted with his views and it was a terrible disappointment to some of them when he compromised over the matter. Two who studied Latin, Hebrew and Greek with him in 1522-1523, were Grebel and Mantz.[2] Mantz (1498-1527) was the obvious man to become Hebrew tutor at Zurich, but Zwingli declined to give him the position because of his radical theological tendencies. Conrad Grebel, son of a wealthy merchant who was one of the most influential magistrates in Zurich, had the advantage of an excellent education at Basle and Paris. A playboy, he did not make good until his marriage in 1522. This displeased his father, who cut him off, since he felt that he married below his station. Family responsibilities had a sobering effect upon Grebel who in due course experienced evangelical conversion. Zwingli's exposition of the Greek text was partly instrumental in this change. Grebel and Mantz, who knew Zwingli well, and who benefited from his ministry, were later to suffer for their convictions as we shall see.

There were several other men of note who desired Radical Reformation, including Reublin, a preacher in the villages of Wytikon and Zollikon. In 1522 Reublin became the first Roman priest to marry. Haetzer, Hubmaier and Blaurock, all ex-priests and well equipped intellectually, were other influential characters involved in the Anabaptist movement in the Zurich area.

As we look more closely at Hubmaier (1481-1528) we will be in a better position to appreciate the situation of those days.

After study under John Eck at Freiburg University, where he made rapid progress, receiving his doctorate in theology, Hubmaier was ordained into the priesthood. Being a full-blooded Roman Catholic it is with regret that it is to be noted that he played an ignoble part in persecuting Jews at Regensberg where the synagogue was burned down. However, he became disillusioned with Roman practice and feeling his way toward the evangelical position, was glad to receive a call to Waldshut, a village

[1] For further details see *Verduin*, p. 199.
[2] See *Williams*, p. 93.

situated just outside Switzerland, not far from Zurich. By 1524 Waldshut was evangelically reformed under his ministry. It is noteworthy that Hubmaier appeared at the second Zurich disputation in October 1523, where with Haetzer, Mantz and Grebel he argued against the Mass.[1] At this disputation Zwingli temporised, not wishing to divide the canton. Consequently he disappointed his friends. They felt that he had compromised by committing the Reformation into the hands of the civil authorities. As time went on the rift deepened. In conventicles (private religious gatherings) in the environs of Zurich the issues became clear.

The radical Christians interpreted Zwingli's Reform as a replacement of one civil order with another. In other words, Papal Christendom was being replaced with Protestant Christendom, the magistrates being the major instruments in the change-over. The idea of a separated church, free from the jurisdiction of both prelates and magistrates, seemed to be set on one side. The dissenters sought a gathered church of believers and this idea crystallised in the first baptism, when Grebel baptised Blaurock in the home of Mantz on January 21, 1525.[2] In the weeks preceding this event, on two successive Tuesdays, January 10 and 17, 1525, Grebel, Mantz and Reublin had discussed baptism with Zwingli and Bullinger. This was known as the First Baptismal Disputation. Several were won over to believers' baptism but the Council soon afterwards reaffirmed its position in regard to infants by passing a decree that all who failed to have their offspring baptised within eight days would be banished. Evening gatherings in the homes of the dissenters continued, and represented the first informal beginnings of gathered Baptist churches in the area. In the course of the week following the first baptism thirty-five were baptised by affusion (pouring) at Zollikon, which was followed by the Lord's Supper, both bread and wine being distributed in an informal celebration of apostolic simplicity. This was in marked contrast to the ritual ceremony of the Mass.

Mantz and Blaurock in particular were powerful preachers. They laid great stress on repentance and the Great Commission. Deep conviction of sin attended the movement, which spread rapidly. Restrictions imposed by the authorities upon preaching activities were ignored. The magistrates were soon to prevail however, with increasing power and severity.

In the meantime Hubmaier had been dedicating infants at Waldshut, in lieu of baptising them. He had written to Oecolampadius at Basle, contending against paedobaptism in lucid terms. "I know," he declared, "that it will not go well with Christendom, until Baptism and the Supper are brought back to their original purity."[3] Oecolampadius had replied disapprovingly, by quoting Augustine that the faith of the parents suffices

[1] Described in detail by *Williams*, p. 90.

[2] ibid., pp. 118-120.

[3] We do well to ponder this profound statement.

17

for infants. In April 1525 Hubmaier and sixty others were baptised by Reublin. Hubmaier in the days following baptised over 300, whereupon he wrote to Zwingli desiring to debate the issue of believers' baptism. Earlier, on May 1, 1523, Hubmaier had conferred with Zwingli. Referring later to this he declared: "Then and there you (Zwingli) said that I was right in saying that children should not be baptised before they were instructed in the faith; this had been the custom previously, therefore such were called catechumens. You promised to bring this out in your exposition of the Articles, as you did in the 18th Article of Confession. Anyone who reads will find therein your opinion clearly expressed."[1] It is important to note that Hubmaier, unlike his Swiss brethren, sought the sanction and support of evangelical magistrates. The Zurich Council apparently ignored Hubmaier's request for a debate. In November 1525 we find Grebel, Mantz and Blaurock imprisoned. Hubmaier, who was formerly part of the Magisterial Reformation and hence more secure, went to Zurich to try and save the Radical Reformation by pleading with Zwingli. G. H. Williams describes his attitude at this point as "Quixotic". He did not have a hope, as events were soon to prove.

From this point the situation only hardened. Hubmaier was cast into prison and tortured. A new mandate threatening death to anyone re-baptising was issued. Mantz was condemned to perish by drowning, and became the first "Protestant" martyr to die at the hands of Protestants on January 5, 1527. His end was brave. He praised God on the way to execution and his last words were the same as his Lord's and Stephen's. Blaurock escaped lightly by comparison, being stripped to the waist and beaten out of the city with rods. Hubmaier was forced to recant, by means of the rack, and then allowed to leave Zurich. Several notable persons were converted to believers' baptism by Hubmaier after this time. But persecution was mounting, and in January 1528 he was burned alive. Encouraged by his wife, a person of outstanding valour, he kept up his spirits by repeating the scriptures to himself on the way to the stake. His last utterance was "O Jesus, Jesus". A few days later, his wife was thrown into the Danube with a stone tied about her neck.

What of Grebel?[2] He had died of the plague in prison in Zurich in 1527. Few of these men were permitted to reach any degree of experience and some of them died at a very young age. Most, if not all, of the potential leaders, were cut off before they could develop depth and maturity of judgment. Such was Michael Sattler, a talented young man, who at the age of 29 in 1527 had his tongue torn out, his body lacerated with red hot tongs and then burned. His wife perished in the same way as Hubmaier's wife. *Let us remember that the state-church system rather than the*

---

[1] B. J. Kidd, *Documents of the Continental Reformation.*

[2] By using the indices the stories of these men can be traced in *Williams.* Various research articles have also been consulted. It is a pity that wholehearted recommendation of some works is not possible due to the modernistic views of the authors.

Reformers was responsible for these gruesome events. The ugliness of recent events in Northern Ireland reminds us that human nature is not changed by state religion or parties. The pattern of what happened at Zurich was repeated more or less at other centres such as St. Gall and Berne. But our study would be incomplete if we did not consider the great reformer of Geneva.

Calvin

Calvin did not have as much contact with the Anabaptists as did Zwingli, although he married Idolette de Bure, widow of John Stordeur. Stordeur had confessed "his crime" of Anabaptism and had gone over to the Reformed party. Calvin was horrified at the numerical extent and influence of the Anabaptists. He devoted one of his earliest works to the refutation of an error common among them namely, psychopannychia (soul-sleep). This was published in 1544. Calvin's last personal encounter with evangelical Anabaptism seems to have taken place in 1546, with the arrival at Geneva of one Belot, a colporteur. The prevailing stringent policy against Anabaptists was immediately applied, and Belot was arrested, whereupon Calvin intervewed him. We have only Calvin's description to go by but he mockingly caricatures Belot as "giving himself with raised head and rolling eyes the majestic aspect of a prophet". We can well understand how an unfortunate impression of Belot confirmed Calvin's bad impression of Anabaptists, to whom he refers in his Institutes as "furious madmen".

Subsequent trends

Thus we have seen that the gulf between the Anabaptists and the Reformers widened to irrevocable proportions. From 1535 to 1546 in Friesland alone, no less than 30,000 Baptists were put to death, Romans and Protestants joining in the butchery. "It can be safely said," declares the historian Dr. Rufus Jones, "that no other movement for spiritual freedom in the history of the Church has such an enormous martyrology." In Germany, particularly, the Baptist cause was thoroughly suppressed, so that it never amounted to anything of significance until Johann Oncken (1800-1884) pioneered a Baptist work in which he eventually overcame intense opposition and persecution. By 1950 there were 559 Baptist churches with a total of over 100,000 members. In England, however, the spiritual descendents of the left wing gained a permanent foothold and, as Bainton points out, "did even more than the Established Church to fashion the temper of England and America".[1]

To refer to areas beyond the Continent is consistent since the ecclesiastical pathway structured by the Reformers was to be trodden elsewhere. The Reformation of the church brought deliverance from Popery and superstition on a scale beyond calculation. It was, however, a road which radical

[1] *Studies in the Reformation*, p. 129.

Christians could not tread and Baptists in England suffered in the same way as did their brethren on the Continent. Protestantism has treasured the memory of her martyrs: sometimes we have been reminded that there were Roman Catholic martyrs as well. During 1970 the Pope canonised 40 English Roman Catholic martyrs of the 16th century. But buried under the dust of that era, unheralded and forgotten, lie large numbers of English Baptists who died for their faith. Spurgeon, in his colourful way tells the story of one of the early Baptist martyrs:

Jane Bouchier, our glorious Baptist martyr, the maid of Kent, when she was brought before Cranmer and Ridley, was able to nonplus them entirely; of course we believe part of her power lay in the goodness of the subject, for if there be a possibility of proving infant baptism by any text in the Bible, I am sure I am not aware of the existence of it; Popish tradition might confirm the innovation, but the Bible knows no more of it than the baptism of bells and the consecration of horses. But, however, she answered them all with a singular power—far beyond what could have been expected of a countrywoman. It was a singular instance of God's providential judgment that Cranmer and Ridley, two bishops of the church who condemned this Baptist to die, said when they signed the death-warrant, that burning was an easy death, and they had themselves to try it in after days; and that maid told them so. She said, "I am as true a servant of Christ as any of you; and if you put your poor sister to death, take care lest God should let loose the wolf of Rome on you, and you have to suffer for God too."[1]

To summarise the account so far. We have seen how the idea of a gathered church was seriously considered by Luther in 1520, but how a decade later he was committed completely to the sacral system, even to the point of agreeing to the death penalty for Baptists. The influence of the Zwickau fanatics undoubtedly assisted to discredit the Baptist view in Luther's mind. In the case of Zwingli, we have a man who faced an agonising choice. He chose the way of magisterial reformation. His friends who went in the other direction perished and with them the brightest hopes ever fostered for a Baptist share in the Reformation. By the time we come to Calvin the lines are set, Bullinger and Oecolampadius being confirmed paedobaptists. It is doubtful whether Calvin ever entertained any serious thought that the Baptists might be right. The contact he did have with them seemed only to confirm his convictions that the Baptists as a whole were just misguided pests.

Despite the spread of the concept of religious freedom, the threat of sacralism is still with us today in the form of the ecumenical movement, with its quest for one, united, universal Church of the world. This is an exceedingly dangerous movement and it is lamentable that evangelicals should be found giving it support. During the last century Dr. Francis Wayland, a Baptist author, expressed the danger of sacralism in vivid terms as follows:

A church organised after the manner of civil commonwealth may retain its form long after the last vestige of piety has vanished and continue for ages as an enemy of Christ and a persecutor of the saints. The soil of Christendom at the present day is covered with the festering carcasses of churches from which the Spirit has

[1] *New Park Street*, 1860, p. 481.

for generations departed. The moral atmosphere is rendered pestilential by their presence and neither piety nor humanity can breathe it and survive.[1]

Conclusions

The main application is clear. In contrast to the Old Testament idea of a national territorial church, Baptists believe that a radical change has taken place with the coming of the New Covenant. In contrast with the national territorial idea, Baptists believe in a gathered church in which every member knows the Lord "from the least of them to the greatest of them" (Jer. 31: 34).

It is necessary to confirm our union with the Reformers in all aspects of their theology—infant-sprinkling and sacralism excepted. It is the core of Luther's evangelical experience, his rejection of free will, his belief in predestination, his clear formulation of justification by faith alone, through grace alone, upon the authority of Scripture alone, that unites us in spirit to him.

We admire Calvin for his great example of exegeting Scripture, and we are thankful for his commentaries and his Institutes. With Spurgeon, we acknowledge our great debt to the Puritans for their rich expositions of the grace of God. Speaking for myself, I have greater unity with a paedobaptist minister who loves the doctrines of grace, than with a Baptist pastor whose ministry is stunted through shallowness and lack of doctrine. Unhappily, Liberalism has increased among Baptists, and needless to say, once a minister denies the fundamentals of the faith, Christian fellowship is no longer possible. While not ready to join formally with a sacral church, I would, for the benefit of the whole family, rather attend one such, where expository preaching was maintained, than endure so much that is infantile and dishonouring in some Baptist churches where the concepts of God and his sovereignty fall far below what Scripture sets forth.

It is necessary to assert these sentiments boldly, since our formulation of a clear doctrine of baptism and of the nature of the church is based squarely on what we commonly call the Reformed Faith. The name "Reformed Baptists" is sound, since it conveys the true position, namely, that we embrace Reformed theology in every aspect except for believers' baptism and all that goes with that by way of a gathered believing church. Moreover, wherever possible, we should call the orthodox evangelical Anabaptists of the Reformation "Baptists" and not "Anabaptists". As far as we are concerned, paedobaptism is no baptism. Therefore the question of re-baptism does not arise. Indeed our greatest objection to paedobaptism is that it destroys believers' baptism. Modern Roman Catholic Spain illustrates this. Reformed paedobaptists working there acknowledge (and herein they are consistent with themselves) the validity of Roman Catholic infant baptism. This concept, if followed in practice,

[1] *The Principles of the Baptists*, Bunyan Lib., 1861.

means that believers' baptism is never witnessed and as a general rule we might say of paedobaptist churches as a whole that they simply have no idea of the meaning of believers' baptism as practised in the New Testament. Never having been baptised as believers themselves, their aversion for the ordinance is often as great as is our love for it.

Because of our union with them in regard to the main body of truth, it behoves us to present our position in a way which shows that we have taken all their reasoning into account. Recently I had fellowship with an Anglican who seceded from the Church of England after ten years as a vicar. I found I had union with him in every aspect of the faith, except baptism. We have been corresponding over the matter, and in reply to one of my letters he wrote as follows: "I could not agree with you more when you say the last thing we want is cleavage. Already I can see that this one issue is dividing Reformed Christians and I cannot but feel that this division will be a great hindrance to the Lord's work in the future."

My view is that this is not a hindrance while we agree to differ in an amicable spirit. This is better than attempting an amalgam which does not work in practice. A paedobaptist cannot wholeheartedly insist upon the baptism of converts as did Peter the apostle, at least not in our society where indiscriminate baptism is recognised. We cannot accept this as valid and cannot compromise here, since that is to compromise the nature of the local church in a radical way. Moreover, baptism is not an intellectual matter merely; it is interwoven with true repentance.

The position has not been helped in the past on account of the attitude assumed by some Reformed paedobaptists who have tended to regard Baptists as sub-Reformed and "unenlightened", on account of their presumed inability to understand the implications of the Covenant. Admittedly, this unfortunate attitude has often been encouraged by the fact that so many Baptists have been superficial in doctrine, and because Particular Baptists who hold consistent views of the Covenant have been a minority. The great majority of Baptists today are of Arminian persuasion and hence are in no position to impress Reformed paedobaptists with their arguments.

The case for Reformed Baptists is much clarified by David Kingdon's book, *Children of Abraham*.[1]

It is not, however, just for the sake of better relationships among the Reformed that we need the clearest expressions of believers' baptism. Pastors are required by the terms of their office in the ministry to teach their people in such a way that there is no doubt about the matter. Believers' baptism, and the union with Christ that it expresses, is so intimately bound up with the doctrine of the church that we cannot afford to be obscure about it.

Let us guard against lowering our estimate of the Reformers or of the

[1] Carey Publications.

Reformation because of sacralism which harmed the Baptists then, and which has tended to make them suspicious of Reformed teaching as a whole ever since, thus depriving them of great theological riches. Basic human factors, as we have seen, influenced Luther, Zwingli and Calvin. They acted within the context of their times. As we are called to act within ours, we do well to seek a grasp of truth as profound as theirs, combining that with the main facet for which the Baptists contended, namely, that the Church of Christ upon earth is to consist only of those who meet the requirements of the New Covenant—a new heart and a new spirit.

Interest in the history of the Baptists in England is increased when tourists in England come across old Baptist churches which can trace their origin back to the seventeenth century. Some of these causes have fallen by the wayside. Others have been revived during the last decade. The old Baptist Chapel, Bradford on Avon, is one such. This cause began in 1662, the year of the Great Ejection, when some two thousand ministers were ejected from the Church of England. The present building was erected in 1789. The existence of such churches up and down the country enhances the value of history and makes our heritage more relevant.

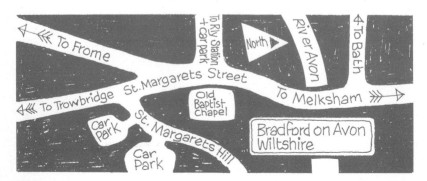

ENGLISH
BAPTIST HISTORY

TWO distinct groups of Baptists emerged during the seventeenth century in England, the General Baptists and the Particular Baptists. The General Baptists were the first to arise and had their origin in John Smyth (d. 1612) who had strong Puritan leanings. Persecution drove him and his Separatist church to Amsterdam from Gainsborough in 1608. Smyth strove hard to build his church according to the New Testament pattern and his study of the Scriptures brought him to practise believers' baptism. Common ground brought contact with the Mennonites with whom he sought union which caused the separation from him of Thomas Helwys and several others who returned to London in 1612 to establish the first Baptist Church in England. This church was Arminian in doctrine. Smyth died the same year having suffered a prolonged illness. His writings were significant and included a long and detailed Confession of Faith in which we can see to what extent he departed from the Calvinism of the English Separatists. It is highly probable that Smyth was the first to claim full religious liberty in England, as found in article 84 of his Confession of Faith. Helwys died in prison in 1616 and was succeeded by John Murton. By 1630 there were six congregations. These corresponded with and sought fellowship with the Mennonites of the Continent.

The Particular Baptists, so called because of their belief in a definite or particular atonement, in which Christ died specifically and only for his elect people, arose through secession from a Calvinistic Independent Church whose theology they retained. This Church was none other than the first Congregational Church founded by Henry Jacob (1553-1624) which later became known as the Jacob-Lathrop-Jessey church after the succession of Puritan pastors.

The first congregation of Particular Baptists can be traced to between 1633 and 1638 with John Spilsbury (1593-1668) as the pastor.[1]   Baptist

[1] Due mainly to scarcity of source material historians differ in regard to some of these dates.   Some are prepared to be more dogmatic than others.   For instance, John Clifford's, *History of Baptists*, gives date of first church as 12.9.1633.

convictions are close to the concept of the local church held by Independents. Believers' baptism dovetails with the idea of a gathered separated body of the faithful. It is not surprising therefore that further secessions from the Independents took place in which, happily, resentment and rancour were markedly absent. In 1645, Hanserd Knollys (1599-1691), a Puritan who seceded from Anglicanism, became pastor of one Particular Baptist Church, William Kiffin (1616-1701), a successful and wealthy merchant, being the pastor of another. The influence of Knollys and Kiffin brought a third to accept Reformed theology. His name also begins with "K", Benjamin Keach (1640-1704). He was a General Baptist whose title to fame rests largely on the fact that he is reputed to be the first to introduce hymn singing into worship and also because he was the second minister at Southwark in the long line of Calvinistic ministers at that church leading up to Spurgeon.

Growth was steady so that by 1660 there were about 131 Particular Baptist Churches and 115 of General Baptist persuasion. Increase continued until 1689 when Parliament passed the Act of Toleration. Although this Act did not grant full religious liberty it certainly made things much easier for non-conformists. But an alarming indifference to spiritual things soon began to prevail and sluggishness overcame the churches.

During the first half of the 18th century many of the General Baptists lapsed by way of Arianism into sheer Unitarianism, while in the same period hyper-Calvinism began to raise its ugly head among the Particular Baptists.

It is significant that doctrinal standards soon disappeared among the General Baptists so that there was nothing to prevent them from drifting into error during this period when adverse winds were blowing. In contrast to this the Particular Baptists were doctrinally minded. Both groups had published confessions but the General Baptists were so weak doctrinally that as early as 1697 they could not even commit churches to a clear statement on the Trinity, whereupon seven Midland churches withdrew from the General Baptist Association.

The first Particular Baptist Confession was published in 1644. It was revised in 1646 and presented to Parliament. It consists of 52 articles, is strongly Calvinist and clearly asserts believers' baptism by immersion. It also restricts the Lord's Supper to baptised believers.

In 1677 there met an assembly of pastors and elders and as a result of their deliberations a second and fuller Confession of Faith was published. It was not signed at this stage, but twelve years later it was republished by the General Assembly of 1689. For this reason it is usually referred to as the 1689 Confession. The introduction to the 1677 edition stated that it is a modification of the Westminster Confession and also of the Savoy Declaration, "to convince all that we have no itch to clog religion with new words, but do readily acquiesce in that form of sound words, which hath been in consent with the Holy Scriptures, used by others before us". Apart from those sections which deal with Baptism and Church Government, the harmony with the Westminster Confession is very close indeed. This Confession of 1689 thus helps to emphasise the spiritual unity of those who held the Reformed Faith at this time and later. A small but important group amongst the early Particular Baptists practised open communion and so nothing was said about restriction of the Supper to baptised believers, but the case was argued for believers' baptism, in an extended appendix, rejecting the contention that infant baptism is for the New Covenant what circumcision was for the Old. Circumcision was "suited only for the male children, baptism is an ordinance suited for every believer, whether male or female". This Confession was endorsed by representatives of over a hundred churches who met in 1689. Among those who signed the 32 articles were Knollys, Kiffin and Keach. Spurgeon republished the 1689 Confession in the second year of his London ministry in 1855, pointing out in his preface that "for between 150 and 200 years it had remained the definitive Confession of Faith of the Particular Baptist churches of England and Wales". He went on to describe it as "the ancient gospel of martyrs, confessors, reformers and saints". The 1689 Confession was again republished in 1958, the year when revival of interest in Reformed theology really began to accelerate. Thus we can trace an unbroken line of Baptist belief in the Puritan doctrines expressed at Westminster in 1646, 1677, 1689 and on to 1958. The most recent edition of the 1689 Confession is dated 1966. In the same year the Strict Baptists published *We Believe*, an Affirmation of Faith based in many respects upon the 1689 Confession, endorsing all its teaching with some modern application. In 1975 Carey Publications published *A Faith to Confess* being the 1689 Confession rewritten in modern English by Mr. S. M. Houghton, together with an introduction designed to increase the usefulness of the Confession for church members. The 1689 Confession was adopted by the Calvinistic Baptists of North America in 1744, and called by them the Philadelphia Confession of Faith.

From this sketch we observe that Continental Anabaptist influence was confined to the early General Baptists who had some contact with the Mennonites but whose genesis must be traced to Puritan stock.

The Particular Baptists stemmed from the Reformation and apart from Baptism have held to Reformed teaching through the years. Since the turn of the present century a serious decline in doctrinal standards has taken place, but during the last fifteen years a revival of interest in books by Reformers, Puritans and Presbyterians has multiplied in many different areas. Increasingly a heritage of Reformed Baptist literature is being brought to light and awaits publication.

We should note at the beginning that, through the centuries and during these last few years, Particular Baptists have been children of the Reformation. They have followed the Reformers and Puritans in the main

John Bunyan

body of truth and hence are true heirs of the Reformation. They have, however, rejected infant baptism as well as sacralism. In regard to believers' baptism, the concept of the gathered local church consisting of saints, and on the question of religious liberty they have kinship with the despised Anabaptists of the 16th century who, for all their faults, did, for the most part, see these matters in a clear light.

At this point I would like to illustrate the history of the Particular Baptists in the British Isles by outlining the outstanding personalities. These are undoubtedly Bunyan, followed by Gill, then, clustered together, Fuller and Carey, Ryland, Pearce and Booth; then Alexander Carson and the Haldane brothers, and finally, the most famous of all, Charles Haddon Spurgeon.

John Bunyan, 1628-1688

If Spurgeon outstrips all others for the number of printed sermons circulated, Bunyan has no rival for the popularity of his world classic *The Pilgrim's Progress*, now translated into over 120 languages. Every Christian can see himself portrayed to some degree in Bunyan's famous allegory. As with Luther before him and Spurgeon after, Bunyan's grasp of the sovereign grace of God can be attributed to the deep conviction of sin that gripped his soul, particularly during the early stages of his pilgrimage. His spiritual experience covered the entire keyboard from deepest bass to highest treble. Baptised in the Ouse in 1653, Bunyan soon began to preach and most surely takes his place among the powerful preachers of history. He was well equipped in his personality to enact the graphic passages which we frequently discover in his writings. A perusal of a recorded sermon such as the one entitled "A few sighs from Hell" should prove the point. John Owen, the greatest of Puritan theologians, told Charles II that he would willingly exchange all his learning for the tinker's power of touching men's hearts.

For the odious sin of continuing to preach when forbidden to do so by the magistrates in 1660 he was put in prison where he was kept by his own conscience for a total of twelve years. He could have obtained freedom if prepared to sacrifice principle. Separation from his family caused him acute suffering, yet out of gall came sweetness in the form of his most edifying writings. Bunyan's works, edited by George Offor were published in three large volumes in 1854. These writings reflect a very happy proportion of doctrine, experience and practical application. The energy of Bunyan's evangelistic thrust is sometimes terrific but the tenderness and beauty of the Gospel is always reflected and seen even in the titles of the expositions such as "Come and welcome to Jesus Christ". Bunyan typifies some of the most admirable features which adorn Baptist history as follows:

1. He was pre-eminently a man of the Book, biblical to the marrow.

2. He stressed doctrine, experience and practice in the best proportions typical of the Puritan era in which he lived. 3. He was a mighty preacher whose eloquence was the gift of the Holy Ghost. 4. He was not embittered by persecution. 5. God rendered his service immortal in spite of his poverty and lack of education. Like Carey and Abraham Booth he was self-taught. 6. Unlike many of much greater learning, God gave the tinker an inspired aptitude for what we now call "communication". His imaginative, lively allegories and illustrations touch the innermost chords of the human heart. Christmas Evans (1766-1838), later Baptist preacher of great power, was nicknamed the "Welsh Bunyan" because he shared Bunyan's mastery of parabolic comparison and dramatic presentation. An enquiry into why these gifts have disappeared would be of no small profit.

John Gill, 1697-1771

John Bunyan, although a separatist and despite his unusual features, was typical of the Puritans. He stands in marked contrast to Gill who lacked his evangelical warmth and urgency. But it would be a mistake to underrate Gill or bypass him. He forms a watershed in the Particular Baptist movement which was to develop another stream with its own features along hyper-Calvinist lines. But let us look at John Gill the man. By the age of eleven Gill had gained a basic knowledge of Latin and Greek. His school studies terminated at this age because his non-conformist parents refused to agree to compulsory attendance for the boys at the Grammar School. Gill's thirst for learning was insatiable and he studied privately, gaining a knowledge of Hebrew, philosophy and logic among several other subjects. He was converted at nineteen and baptised. Soon afterwards he began to preach. In 1719 at the age of 22 he was called to the church at Southwark which was to become famous for its succession of famous ministers: Benjamin Keach, Benjamin Stinton, Gill, John Rippon and Spurgeon. Gill served the Southwark church for 52 years, and Rippon who followed him for 63 years, 115 years between them. In his four-volume autobiography Spurgeon tells the story of his predecessors in scintillating fashion.

Gill excelled in the Rabbinical learning by which he obtained his Aberdeen doctorate. A profound and comprehensive theologian and prolific writer he produced his first commentary, a work on the Song of Solomon, in 1724 (published 1728), which led to his writing a massive commentary on the whole Bible. To this was added a three-volume Body of Divinity and a work defending Calvinism in four volumes with the title *The Cause of God and Truth*. With regard to Calvinism, Toplady said of him, "Certainly no man has treated that momentous subject, the system of divine grace in all its branches, more closely, judiciously, and successfully". Gill vigorously opposed infant baptism as he did the Arminianism of John Wesley.

As we look closely at his life and works we find that theologically he mingled with high Calvinists and you will look in vain for references to men at lower Calvinistic levels. Although these names may not be familiar to us now it is noteworthy that Gill's friendship was with Richard Davis, John Skepp, and John Brine who were all hyper-Calvinists. His preferences in literature lay in the direction of Tobias Crisp and the orthodox men of Holland such as Witsius, but also happily with Thomas Goodwin and John Owen. Gill's failure lay not so much in what he said but in what he omitted to say. Had he followed John Owen's line he would have surely ranked amongst the greatest theologians. He certainly was one of the most learned men the Baptists have ever produced. Unhappily he restricted the Gospel by failing to beseech the unconverted to be converted to God. To fail to do justice to scriptures which highlight man's responsibility to believe and repent and to suppress the gracious invitations of Christ to all men is to deprive the word "Gospel" of its real meaning. Invitations and exhortations are to the Gospel what heaters are to cold buildings in an English winter. Turn them off and the people freeze. While Gill's weaknesses should be noted that we might avoid them ourselves let us also observe his strengths. His mammoth commentary, verse by verse on the whole Bible reminds us that he was a man of iron discipline always pressing perseveringly forward with his pen. Christ endues his servants with different gifts and no one could deny that John Gill used his writing ability to the full. For instance his *Body of Divinity* is carefully set out and full of excellent matter. Some rank his commentary on the Song of Solomon as the best to be had.

Hyper-Calvinism largely explains why it took some time for the evangelical awakening of the 18th century to have effect upon the Particular Baptists. Andrew Fuller was one of the main instruments used to overcome the hyper-Calvinism which had spread among the churches.

Andrew Fuller, 1754-1815

Fuller was brought up under preaching of the Gill type. "The minister," he wrote later, "had seldom anything to say except to believers." When Fuller came under intense conviction of sin at the age of fifteen all the minister could say was, "attend the means of grace, and may the Lord call you by it in due time". Fuller reckons he might have found relief from his soul's agony had he known that he needed no preliminary qualifications for coming to Christ. When he overcame his difficulties he was baptised in 1770. Eighteen months later he came across a gross instance of antinomianism which is a plant that grows well in the soil of hyper-Calvinism. A church member had been guilty of drunkenness and excused the sin by saying that he could not help himself. Fuller reasoned with the man but was reprimanded on account of his youth. The whole church became involved and eventually called on the minister to resign because he supported Fuller who claimed that we are responsible for our actions and that we are not stocks and stones.

The church situated at the Elephant and Castle in London, known as Spurgeon's Tabernacle, or the Metropolitan Tabernacle, has an unrivalled history.   Dr. John Gill was the minister for fifty-two years of the congregation which in his day met in Carter Lane.   The diagram on pages 40-41 shows the history of this church which in 1971 was taken out of the Baptist Union under the leadership of Peter Masters who became the pastor in 1970.

At the age of 21 Fuller became pastor of the church in Soham, moving from there to Kettering seven years later. Early in his ministry he received much help from the writings of Bunyan and Gill. He soon detected the difference between the two. Both believed in predestination but Bunyan, in contrast to Gill, believed in the free offers of the Gospel. At first Fuller concluded that Bunyan was in error but after further prayerful thought and study he was convinced that Bunyan was right after all. In 1776 he began to exhort the unconverted to repent of sin and believe in Christ. His flock was not impressed and this was one of the main reasons why he left Soham for Kettering in 1782.

These exercises in the question of divine sovereignty and human responsibility extended Fuller in further study, prayer and research. He began to collate his notes. This gave rise to a manuscript to which he gave the title *The Gospel Worthy of All Acceptation*. He feared to publish it but friends prevailed upon him. Appearing in 1784 it caused an immediate storm. The hyper-Calvinists fired a broadside from one side and the General Baptists raked him with gunshot from the other. By now Fuller had come to detest both hyper-ism and Arminianism. He was well and truly fixed in the saddle of Puritan theology without any danger of falling off front, back or sides. His theology was soundly scriptural and sanely balanced and he held the antinomy of Predestination and Responsibility with an iron grasp. He had nothing in common with the shallow notions of free-willers and writing to Dr. Ryland he said, "If my present connection (the Particular Baptists) were to disown me I should rather choose to go through the world alone than be connected with them (the Arminian Baptists)."

Fuller's book, opening up the whole question of the moral responsibility of sinners in regard to the Gospel, was mightily used in his day and has been a blessing ever since. His pen was both fluent and versatile and he wrote on a variety of subjects exposing the errors of his day. One of his best works was an Exposition of Genesis which Spurgeon rated highly, describing it as "weighty, judicious and full of Gospel truth".

Fuller served as secretary of the Particular Baptist Missionary Society from its inception in 1792 to the day of his death in 1815. The extent of his work was tremendous. He was tireless in his efforts to promote what must be regarded as Britain's first proper missionary society. The influence of this society in stimulating missionary interest and inspiring the commencement of other such societies cannot be computed. T. E. Watson in an excellent paper on Fuller's conflict with hyper-Calvinism given at the Puritan Conference of 1959 has this to say, "It is no exaggeration to say that Carey's going to India was the logical outcome of Fuller's emancipation from hyper-Calvinism. Fuller maintained that the Gospel was worthy of *all* acceptation, from which Carey deduced that its acceptance ought to be pressed on *all* mankind."

Rippon, Pearce and Booth

These three outstanding men ought to be mentioned as those responsible for adding brightness to the Particular Baptist scene towards the end of the 18th century. John Rippon (1751-1836) did sterling work in building up the church at Southwark which was beginning to decline when Gill died in harness in 1771. Rippon's life teaches us, however, that there is a time to retire from office. Fine man that he was, he nevertheless continued too long. This had a deleterious effect not only upon the patience of the congregation but also upon its size. Samuel Pearce (1766-99) by contrast burned himself out at 33 but not before he had baptised 335 in nine years in his ministry at Birmingham. For holiness of life and intense devotion to Christ, Pearce was similar to M'Cheyne. History requires that we mention Abraham Booth (1734-1806). Whereas Fuller came down from hyper-Calvinism, Booth came up from Arminianism and these two deserve to be regarded as worthy to take their place alongside the most useful theologians in the Puritan stream from the days of Manton and Flavel on to Spurgeon. Here we find that beautiful blend of doctrine, experience and practice which is the priceless characteristic of Puritan tradition. Booth, son of a small-holder, made his way into life as a weaver. He taught himself Latin and Greek, read deeply into history and waded chest high into the Puritans, John Owen being the favourite. Unlike so many who merely copy others, Booth used his gift of a clear logical mind and retentive memory to develop an independent judgment of his own. But here again, unlike some who have done this only to produce unscriptural novelties, Booth was biblical from top to toe. He wrote many helpful books including a treatise on baptism. His most popular book for reprinting has been *The Reign of Grace*.

Bridging the gap between these men and Spurgeon we must remember Alexander Carson and the Haldane brothers.

Alexander Carson, 1776-1844

At the early age of eighteen, Carson graduated from the University of Glasgow having taken top place in his large class. He immediately entered the Presbyterian ministry in Northern Ireland at Tubbermore, a village of 2,000 people. Here he was to minister for nearly 50 years. As is customary in most Presbyterian churches an outward profession was considered adequate and efforts to discipline slack members were of little avail. Racing, cockfighting and dancing were the rage and Carson did not hesitate to ride into the throng at the race track to remonstrate with his people. He appealed to the Presbytery for support in the matter of discipline but they consistently held to the view that allegiance to the Westminster Confession was all he could demand. Convinced that none but true believers were to be granted the privileges of Church membership, Carson resigned from the Presbytery. This alienated his wealthy father-in-law and in terms of this world's goods he paid dearly for his convictions.

He continued to preach in the church until the next crisis which arose when some of his members embraced Baptist convictions. He opposed them with vigour and charity but the dispute served to convert him to the Baptist position as well. This really provoked the wrath of the synod and they sent a delegation to evict Carson from the church by force. He appealed to them to allow him to complete his sermon, upon which one of the deacons took the pulpit Bible and exclaimed to the congregation, "Let all who wish to follow the Bible come this way". The place was immediately emptied. They gathered in the fields for services and when winter came met in a barn. Conversions were frequent and eventually the baptised membership totalled 500. Despite their material losses God provided for the Carsons (there were thirteen children) and for the church. The new Presbyterian minister took up the cudgels against Carson but was no match for him, Carson's written works testifying to his ability. Some have wondered why Carson dealt at such lengths and gave such prominence to *Mode* in his classic work *Baptism: its Mode and Subjects*. There are important reasons for this order, one of which is that we have no warrant to begin the study of baptism by studying circumcision. The relationship of baptism to circumcision follows after we have ascertained the nature of baptism itself. Carson wrote other books and helped Robert Haldane with his great commentary on Romans.

The Haldane Brothers: Robert, 1764-1842, James, 1768-1851

The Haldane family for many centuries possessed the barony of Gleneagles and over the years were blessed with many illustrious sons, not least Robert and James both of whom received a handsome education. Robert inherited the estate and throughout his life was known for his discreet and generous support of the work of the Lord to the tune of thousands every year.[1] Both brothers were noted for distinguished and gallant service as officers in the Royal Navy and Robert in later life sometimes described famous battles in which he had taken part. For several years he was engaged in the administration of his large estate until at the age of 30 he was converted, as was his brother in the same year. A godly mother long before had been used to sow the incorruptible seed and it is remarkable that both brothers independently of each other resolved to lay aside the worldly life about the same time. It would seem as one reviews James' career as a captain in the navy that he was made half of oak and half of steel, and it is not surprising to find that his natural gifts —an alert mind, physical courage and determination, combined with spiritual gifts of discernment—helped mould him into a preacher of apostolic order. Three years after his conversion, in 1797, James toured Scotland, preaching in the open air after the style of Wesley and Whitefield. He preached on an average three times a day to assemblies which frequently

---

[1] He gave between £50,000 and £60,000 towards propagating the Gospel at home between 1799 and 1807. What he gave later cannot be computed. *History of Baptists in Scotland*, p. 56.

Andrew Fuller

numbered from 3,000 to 6,000. Glorious conversions attended this ministry. For instance, in one small town visited on the tour 40 solid conversions were accounted for years later.

1798 saw the sale by Robert of the Airthrey estate and the year following James was ordained into the Congregational ministry. A second tour of the North followed.

Robert Haldane, although not possessing the compass or power of voice of his brother, was nevertheless an able preacher. His efforts centred mainly in Edinburgh where he was instrumental in establishing a seminary. Robert built a Tabernacle for his brother in Edinburgh. This seated 3,200, and was opened in July 1801. Here James ministered for nearly 50 years whilst at the same time conducting preaching tours in the North and in Ulster where he had fellowship with Alexander Carson. It should not be thought that Carson's was the only source of influence to persuade the Haldane brothers to become Baptists. Besides a Dr. Stuart in Edinburgh they had fellowship with Andrew Fuller and contributed toward the Serampore Mission. James was baptised in 1805 and announced that he would explain the reasons for his action the next Lord's Day. 4,000 packed the Tabernacle. But he desisted from his design and preached the Gospel, deferring his explanation until the next week. The dignified and wise way in which the Haldane brothers handled the controversy which resulted from their change of view should be noted by those who are in a similar predicament.

The careers of the brothers form a rich tapestry. Of many aspects to which we could advert, two deserve a special place. The visit of Robert Haldane to Geneva in 1816 resulted in a rich harvest in which some of France's most eminent Gospel labourers were established in the truth. Merle d'Aubigné, Malan, Gaussen and Monod are amongst those who could be named. Secondly, the culminating act of Robert's distinguished life was the publication of his superb commentary on Romans. If I may be allowed a word of personal testimony at this point I will say that this commentary first set my feet on the highway to an understanding of the doctrines of grace. We can be sure that countless souls have been strengthened through this commentary which is characterised by the unction and thoroughness that were part of the Haldane brothers.

The early 19th century

The group which associated with Andrew Fuller and included Pearce, Ryland and Carey stood in the tradition of the 1689 Confession. This was true also of Abraham Booth in London and Samuel Medley and John Fawcett in the North of England. During the early 19th century however, changes began to take place. Many Strict Baptists were moving to a more rigidly hyper-Calvinist position, while others in the Particular Baptist group were diluting their Calvinism. This latter development probably owed much to Robert Hall (1764-1831). Hall successively held pastorates in Cambridge, Leicester and Bristol and was considered one of the greatest orators of his day. He, however, rejected belief in the doctrine of Particular Redemption and although he paid tribute to the writings of Richard Baxter and John Howe, despised those of John Owen, whom he described as being "heavy and prolix" as well as being "most illogical". Although Hall was a Baptist he doubted whether any form of church government was laid down in the New Testament and said that he was disposed to adopt the maxim that, "whatever is best administered is best". Robert Hall had a great following and must have helped to promote tendencies among the Baptists that not even Spurgeon was able to check.

C. H. Spurgeon

How poor we Baptists would be without Spurgeon! Like Carey his labours were prodigious in every direction. It would be foolish to attempt the story of Spurgeon here. It should be well-known to us. Reference to some main issues will suffice. When he came to the Southwark church, situated in a most disadvantageous spot, there were only about 80 in the congregation but soon all 1,500 seats were taken. This led not only to extensions which ended in the Metropolitan Tabernacle seating 6,000, but in the hiring of huge auditoriums, such as the Surrey Gardens Music Hall, seating 10,000.

Unlike many who never commit themselves one way or the other Spurgeon declared himself against Arminianism and hyper-Calvinism. Explicit preaching which was doctrinal, expository, experimental, practical, highly topical and absolutely relevant made New Park Street and the Metropolitan Tabernacle, like Westminster Chapel of this century, famous. Good men followed Spurgeon but they lacked that distinctive insistence upon explicit truth which is necessary if the Gospel is to be preserved in purity for future generations. This readiness to contend for the truth brought Spurgeon into controversy. He did not relish conflict and the final battle, known as the downgrade controversy, shortened his life. He showed increasing concern at the compromise among the Particular Baptists (so called even though they had long since left their moorings) who in their quest for unity were prepared to compromise with "the new learning". In the end they were prepared to dilute the truth to such an extent that in 1873 they were unwilling even to contend for the word "evangelical". Spurgeon avowed his beliefs in republishing the 1689 Confession as early as 1855. He always believed that the only adequate basis of faith for the union of churches was one in which the doctrines of grace formed a substantial part. When he saw that this was not possible for the Baptist Union he resigned in 1887. He could not accept that there was any such thing as an undoctrinal Christianity. Writing in the *Sword and Trowel* he declared: "I am unable to sympathise with a man who says he has no creed; because I believe him to be in the wrong by his own showing. He ought to have a creed. What is equally certain, he has a creed—he must have one, even

though he repudiates the notion.   His very unbelief is, in a sense, a creed."
"We are going downhill at breakneck speed," he said, and so it proved,
for in 1891 the General Baptists joined the Baptist Union thus uniting the
two streams for the first time since their inception.

Arminian Baptists

The drift has continued ever since and it is not surprising to find Baptist
Union leaders of our day not only immersed in Ecumenism but also ready
to do business with the Pope of Rome.   This brings us to our application.
Examination of the streams in Baptist history indicates that departures
from the doctrines of the 1689 Confession have led to disaster.

It is true that the Arminian Baptists cannot be accused of departing from
the theology of the 1689 Confession since they never embraced it anyway.
However, their early plunge into Unitarianism illustrates that it is impossible
to survive without clearly defined beliefs.   The majority of Baptist
churches today, like the early Baptist churches, are Arminian in theology.
That is they believe that every person has free will and that God gives
every man a chance to give his heart to Jesus.   Those who choose God
are the elect—God foreknew those who would choose Christ and thus he
elected them.   Success depends upon our endeavours to persuade men to
use their free will.   Hence the emphasis on the altar call and decisions.
In some quarters a preacher is barely regarded as evangelical if he does
not end his sermon with an appeal.   Doctrine is frowned on in many
Arminian churches as something dangerous because it tends to divide
Christians.   Lack of doctrine in Baptist churches everywhere is reflected
in the pubished reports of the *Baptist World Alliance* for the eleventh
congress, held at Miami Beach 1965.   The Alliance reflects the position
of some 33 million Baptists.   The section on Doctrine is as emaciated of
truth as present-day Bangla Desh has been of protein.   The highest note
struck throughout from the doctrinal point of view came from Dr. Billy
Graham, who, quoting some of the great worthies of the past such as
Bunyan, Spurgeon and Carey, went on to cite the Apostles' Creed as their
faith and ours.   This was a noble effort in comparison with the rest, but
as for the doctrines of grace which the old worthies regarded as absolutely
fundamental, they might as well not exist as far as the majority of present-
day Baptists are concerned.   The call goes out constantly to get on with
the business of winning souls.   Now while it is true that we must evangelise,
it is also true that those who are won to Jesus must be built up in gospel
truth and if they are never encouraged to get down to the deep things of
God and to the doctrines, it means we are going to produce a race of
weak, ignorant Christians.   Moreover, a terrible vacuum is created for a
shallow Gospel fails to fill a man's emotional and intellectual needs.

It is not surprising therefore to find that neo-Pentecostalism sweeps into
General Baptist churches.   The modern tongues movement is appallingly
superficial and embraces High Anglicans and Romanists who fail to pass

COMMENTS ON THE CHART

On the right hand side of the chart where recent history is depicted reference is made to The Carey Conference for ministers. This, begun in 1970, has grown in size and influence and is one of several similar expressions of Christian faith and practice in various parts of the world, particularly in the USA. During 1976 it was encouraging to observe the coming together of Strict Baptist ministers with others who represent Reformed Baptist interest from churches independent of the Baptist Union and outside the Strict Baptists. No formal association has been established but spiritual association of a very cordial and helpful kind exists.

The stippled stream representing the church in London where Spurgeon ministered is included because of its remarkable history and because the line of ministry—Rider, Keach, Stinton, Gill, Rippon—has typified particular Baptist history so well.

it is important to note that a diagram of this kind is intended to convey a general idea only. for instance some particular baptists maintain strict communion, arminians are found among strict baptists and calvinists among general baptists.

n.b. the streams are diagrammatic and not necessarily to scale

THE STRICT BAPTISTS — Hyper Calvinism (Gospel Standard)

1. denial that saving faith is the duty of unbelievers (the duty-faith articles)
2. communion restricted to believers of the same faith and order — "strict" communion
3. the gospel, not the moral law the rule of life for believers are found characterising the Gospel Standard Strict Baptists.

JOHN BRINE 1703-1765   WILLIAM GADSBY d1884   J.K. POPHAM 1847-1937

JAMES WELLS d1872

WARBURTON d1857
JOHN KERSHAW 1792-1870
J.C. PHILPOT 1802-1869

S B ministers Conf. 1965
1966 "We Believe" Affirm. of Faith.

THE PARTICULAR BAPTISTS — Calvinism (most of whom practised strict communion)

Henry Jacob d.1624

1644 Part. Bapt. Conf of faith

JOHN GILL 1697-1771

SAMUEL PEARCE

A. FULLER d.1815

A. CARSON

HALDANE BROS

C.H. SPURGEON d.1892   A.W. PINK

new Reformed Baptist interest

Carey Conf. 1970.

ABRH. BOOTH 1734-1806

WILLIAM CAREY d.1834

Rider   Keach   Stinton   John Gill   John Rippon ministers at Southwark

this stream depicts the history of the Southwark church where Spurgeon ministered.

THE GENERAL BAPTISTS — Arminianism

1689 Act of Toleration   1813 Bapt. Union began

1817 ± 70 churches

1612 first Baptist church.

J. SMYTH d.1612
T. HELWYS d.1616

1660 ± 115 churches

MATTHEW. CAFFYN d1714

DAN TAYLOR 1738-1816

new connection 12 churches 1770

JOHN CLIFFORD 1836-1923

merger 1891 inspired by B.U.

Baptist Revival Fellowship

indep. bapt. churches

Unitarianism   1689 Bapt. Confession of Faith .... 1855 republished by Spurgeon. reprinted 1958.   Modernism

1600	10	20	30	40	1650	60	70	80	90	1700	10	20	30	40	1750	60	70	80	90	1800	10	20	30	40	1850	60	70	80	90	1900	10	20	30	40	1950	60	70	72	74	76

| hyper-calvinism | non-baptist influence | Joseph Hussey d1726 | John Skepp. | W. Huntington d.1813 |

| calvinism | Puritans | M. Henry | John Owen | Flavel | G. Whitefield | Tennent | Edwards | Boston | Erskines | C. Hodge | J.C. Ryle | Smeaton | Warfield | Berkhof | Machen | Kuiper |

| arminianism | J. Wesley | Fletcher | C.Finney | D.L. Moody |

the basic Scriptural requirement of Justification by Faith. It is a wonder that Hindus who speak in tongues are not invited to join the cult! Why is this movement so attractive? The answer is that Arminian Christianity has failed to bring believers into a deep experience of the sovereignty and majesty of God. A void has been left and this void must be filled. Many Christians are yearning for reality and neo-Pentecostalism, with its claim to be like apostolic Christianity, seems to be real. Those who are well grounded in the truth are best equipped to discern the shallowness of the teaching.

What about the intellectual vacuum that is created by Arminian Christianity? Many believers, particularly those who have received disciplined intellectual training in universities, are not satisfied with shallow answers to their questions. Arminianism fails to answer their questions. Great areas of truth are avoided and neglected. Frustration results. It is not surprising therefore that Barthianism—neo-orthodoxy—(the old Modernism dressed up in Reformed language) has made some rapid headway among the intellectuals in General Baptist churches. How can these subtle heresies of neo-orthodoxy be resisted when the believers have not been built up in systematic theology? Here is language which purports to deal with God's sovereignty as it relates to the varied spheres of life. It sounds wonderful. But we discover that the advocates of this teaching are universalists who deny the evangelical belief that "All Scripture is God-breathed".

It is tragic that the vacuum left by ignorance is being filled all over the world by that which is not true. Even now, Modernists are being groomed in colleges thought to be evangelical, soon to make their way into evangelical Baptist churches where the poor sheep have never been taught the difference between one system and another.

Strict Baptists

The Strict Baptists have been blessed in the past with preachers of unusual power such as William Gadsby, John Warburton and John Kershaw who could boast of thronged churches. James Wells had a weekly congregation of 2,000. These men were well able to convey the truth of God's glorious holiness, and spoke with an unction that is rare today. However, they were individualists and one very rarely finds that they recommend Puritan authors. Some of them, like James Wells, who opposed Spurgeon, were clear-cut hyper-Calvinists. J. C. Philpot, a seceder from the Church of England and a learned man, was strongly individualistic. He found it necessary to emphasise inward reality of the experience of salvation. Some of his sermons are magnificent in this respect. However, this emphasis has been pressed to an extreme with the result that many have become inordinately introspective. They have looked within to find a warrant to savingly believe, instead of heeding God's command to look

42

to, and savingly believe upon, Jesus Christ. Thus many have never attained assurance.

As the leaders passed from the scene many Strict Baptists have tended to press individualistic characteristics to extremes. The poor state of Arminian churches has not encouraged them and the Gospel Standard group of churches in particular has become exclusive, resisting all inter-communion with other evangelicals. One salutary result has been that Modernism has been shut out and it is hard to find any Strict Baptist preacher anywhere with Modernist views.

The removal of leaders has also resulted in an increase of itinerant preaching. There are literally scores of places with a handful of people going from week to week under an itinerant ministry of a weak character. Destitute of pastoral leadership and oversight many have become so lethargic, introspective and restricted that they have no desire to co-operate with other Christians. The itinerant system in which a man leaves his family responsibilities, travels a considerable distance, delivers an oration or two and then disappears again until the next year is pernicious in the extreme. This system runs counter to all that the New Testament declares about Eldership, shepherding and feeding the flock.

Attempts have been made to change this system by way of two or three men devoting their attention to a single cause instead of travelling about all the time. Way back in 1955 officers and members of Strict Baptist churches met at Chadwell Street, London. It was suggested that pastorless churches should invite itinerant brethren to provide a continuity of ministry for several weeks in one church. The voting was overwhelmingly in favour of the motion, 109 votes for, and four votes against. Many other splendid resolutions were passed in favour of abolishing the itinerant system, but to no effect.

Conclusion

As we look back over the years we see that the balance of theology and practice, doctrine and evangelism is very important. If evangelism is neglected the churches become lifeless. God will have us honour the Great Commission. If we neglect theology, preaching becomes shallow or distorted.

Bunyan, Booth, Carey and Spurgeon are examples of men who maintained an ideal position in respect of theology and evangelism.

It is interesting to note that these leaders were self-taught men without Bible College training. Yet they never despised learning but placed great value on well furnished libraries, having respect for what the Holy Spirit has revealed to others.

The history of Presbyterianism illustrates the importance of an educated ministry. Their preachers have reaped immense advantages from high

Abraham Booth

standards of training. Think of some of the Scottish Presbyterians of the last century whose writing and ministries have enriched the Church at large—George Smeaton, James Buchanan, Patrick Fairbairn, William Cunningham, Rabbi (John) Duncan, John Kennedy, Hugh Martin, David Brown, the Bonar brothers and others. Then there is the Princeton school in the United States leading to Westminster Seminary. We would be much poorer in the theological arena of today without the contributions of Warfield and more recently of E. J. Young, Cornelius van Til and Professor Murray, to name a few leading lights.

It is noteworthy that Andrew Fuller was truly representative not only of the main stream of Particular Baptists but of the Reformed tradition as a whole in holding human inability and responsibility together. Thomas Boston and the Erskine brothers fought a similar battle against hyper-Calvinism and all the above-named leaders would concur with Fuller in his contention that the Gospel is worthy of all acceptation.

Ralph and Ebenezer Erskine and Thomas Boston were nicknamed Marrow-men because they defended the republication of a book entitled *The Marrow of Modern Divinity*. The issue was whether or not there is a universal call to all sinners to receive Christ, with a promise (or offer) of mercy to all that do so. Those who opposed this maintained that only conscious, convicted or contrite sinners have a warrant to come to Christ and only those inwardly prepared are to be called. The Marrow-men asserted that this made the sinners' warrant to believe to hinge on inward qualifications instead of God's command and promise. The Marrow-men sought to defend a universal Gospel offer in which all sinners are obligated to believe having every warrant to do so, being pointed to Christ as an all sufficient saviour.

Theology and Evangelism

The main lesson which emerges is surely the urgent need for another reformation in which theology comes to life. The nature of God, the fall of man, the place of the moral law, the work of the Holy Spirit, the atonement and present reign of Jesus Christ—when these and inter-related themes of revelation become burning issues—in short when theology becomes dynamic, then evangelism will spring forth once more with mighty irresistible power.

Basic to theology becoming alive is conviction of sin and the latter is the result of a realisation of the holiness of God and the meaning of the moral law. This can be illustrated by the life of George Whitefield. As a young man he took ship for America for the first time soon after the Revival had spread in Wales and England. During this voyage God gave him such a sight of his own heart that he wrote to a friend: "I have seen more and more how full of corruption I am", and "God has been pleased to let me see something of my own vileness." He complained of pride and self-love, and prayed "Oh, that these inner conflicts may purify my polluted, proud and treacherous heart." In regard to the sins of his youth he declared, "The remembrance of my past sins overwhelmed my soul, and caused tears to be my meat, day and night."

So great was his conviction of unworthiness that he even contemplated giving up the ministry. His experience was the outcome of his doctrinal belief. During the voyage he wrote to his friend Hervey, "It is sweet to know and preach that Christ justifies the ungodly, and that all truly good works are not so much as partly the cause, but the *effect* of our justification before God. Till convinced of these truths you must own free will in man, which is directly contrary to the Holy Scriptures and the articles of our church."

The doctrines of grace were meat to his soul. "The doctrines of our election, and free justification in Christ Jesus are daily more pressed upon my heart. They fill my soul with a holy fire and afford me great confidence in God my Saviour." He saw these truths as a unity and deplored any separation of them one from another, "I bless God, his Spirit has convinced me of our eternal election by the Father through the Son, of our free justification through faith in his blood, of our sanctification as the consequence of that, and of our final perseverance and glorification as the result of it all. These I am persuaded God has joined together; these, neither men nor devils shall ever be able to put asunder."

This depth of experience which has all but disappeared from the earth is called for today. In other words we need a dynamic theology which results in dynamic evangelism.

BIBLIOGRAPHY

For basic reading I found R. G. Torbet's, *A History of the Baptists* and A. C. Underwood's, *A History of English Baptists*, the most helpful. Underwood does not understand Spurgeon's Calvinism (p. 203 ff.) and those wishing to get to grips with Spurgeon's doctrinal beliefs should read *The Forgotten Spurgeon* by Iain Murray. *A History of the English Baptists*, by Joseph Ivimey in four volumes, forms a treasure house of material. This was published in 1827.

Specialists in Baptist History engaged in research are well advised to consult Edward C. Starr's *A Baptist Bibliography*—which is available for reference at Dr. Williams' Library, 14 Gordon Square, London. This massive work was begun in 1933. Volume 14 has been reached which includes names from Lea to McQuire. References go back to 1609. Anti-Baptist works are also listed. To cite a typical instance of the value of this bibliography the reader can find in it a complete list of all the writings of Abraham Booth and by use of the symbols provided know which Libraries in America and Britain stock the individual items.

THE HISTORY OF BAPTISTS IN AMERICA 1620-1976

IN March 1639, just under twenty years after the Pilgrim Fathers sailed from Plymouth, a simple but historic service took place in the New World. The scene was the new settlement of Providence—now known as Rhode Island—which in three years had attracted 30 immigrant families. This was the service: a certain Ezekiel Hollyman baptised his minister, Roger Williams, whereupon the latter, a Welshman who had been ordained in the Church of England, baptised Hollyman and ten others. Thus the first Baptist Church on American soil was constituted, with the fitting number of twelve disciples.

Today, Baptists in the United States number 29 million.

The growth of America

The large number of Baptists in America is due firstly to early seeds coming to fruition, to revivals which multiplied the converts, and to tremendous endeavour on all fronts thereafter. Indispensable to an understanding of this growth is the factor of population increase. At first progress was slow but the revolutionary war (1776-1783) saw the thirteen colonies emerge as the American Republic established upon a constitution drawn up by eminently gifted leaders. George Washington became the first president in 1789. Under his leadership the country acquired renewed stability and esteem. The story was already one of expansion, but from now on immigration accelerated and the possession of vast tracts of land in the West hastened the process. The Civil War of 1862-1866 was more about Union than about the emancipation of slaves. Union was achieved. The cost in blood and suffering was staggering but America's place as the greatest and wealthiest nation in the world was secured. The streams of immigrants became swollen rivers, until now there is a population of over 200 million. The growth can be seen as follows—1800: 5m, 1850: 23m, 1900: 75m, 1950: 150m. Today besides 29 million Baptists, there are approximately, in millions, 43m Roman Catholics, 14m Methodists, 9m Lutherans, 4m Presbyterians,

James Alexander Haldane

4m Protestant Episcopal and half a million Pentecostals. Baptist growth has kept pace with and at most times exceeded the population growth— that is in proportionate terms!

Three distinct periods emerge as follows:

1 THE OLD WORLD OF TINY BEGINNINGS	1620-1727	Some leading Baptist personalities: Roger Williams John Clarke Henry Dunster John Miles
2 THE PERIOD OF REVIVALS	1727-1860	John Gano Isaac Backus Shubael Stearns Adoniram Judson Luther Rice
3 THE AGE OF HUMAN ORGANISATION	1860-1976	Many gifted men were responsible during this period for expansion in all directions —education, evangelism, missionary endeavour—yet no one prophet of Spurgeon's calibre emerged to uphold the old Reformed faith and effectively withstand the insidious advance of Modernism. In lieu of biographical sketches, we devote this section to application.

1. THE OLD WORLD OF TINY BEGINNINGS: 1620-1727

The struggle for religious freedom in the New England colonies was similar in many ways to that in England although it would be wrong to regard the colonies as merely an extension of England. There has always been a tendency to underestimate the Dutch and German influence and in any case the spirit of independence very soon characterised the New World. Religious predisposition was nevertheless deeply ingrained and while persecution was not as intense as it was in England it was bitter.

The *Mayflower* sailed from Plymouth 350 years ago, an epic in faith and courage but the new Plymouth of 1620 would have been of little significance had it not been for a much greater Puritan migration which took place in the 1630's. To this group belonged Roger Williams. Baptist beginnings cannot be traced back to 1620 although one can say that the spirit of the Mayflower Pilgrims was typical in many ways of the early Baptists of America.

Roger Williams (1600-1685)

Determination and resourcefulness flowed in the veins of this son of Wales. Educated at Pembroke College, Cambridge, he obtained his Bachelor's Degree in 1627, whereupon he entered the ministry of the

Robert Hall

Church of England. He became firmly opposed to the Establishment and was particularly alienated by the antics of Bishop Laud, the arch-persecutor of the Puritans. Williams left Bristol in 1630 and reached Boston February 5, 1631. He became a convinced Separatist in his views and strongly opposed any ties with the Church of England. Ministering among the Congregationalists he soon realised that corruption and persecution were as inevitable in America as in England. He objected to the principle that the magistrate might punish a breach of the first table of the Law—the first four commandments. He began to voice his protest in this regard. The expression of uncompromising views led, in due course, to his banishment from Massachusetts. Such an event might well astonish those who learn it for the first time and so it is well for us to look at the conditions of that time through the eyes of Roger Williams.

The New England Puritans believed firmly in the union of Church and State. They found it necessary to establish their own Civil Government and, by this means, protect themselves as a body from intrusion from without and corruption from within. Conformity was one of the conditions of acceptance in that early society and it was required of all citizens that they give faithful allegiance to the Church. It is a mistake to conclude that these men did not know what religious liberty was all about. They knew it but feared it, for they believed that liberty would lead to anarchy. True freedom, as far as they were concerned, was to be found in the truth as they saw it. This was all very well if you held to all their views, but Roger Williams did not. One writer has put the matter in a facetious way as follows:

> The Puritans came to this country to worship God according to their own consciences, and to prevent other people from worshipping him according to theirn.

However, it would be entirely wrong to belittle these great men. They ought to be respected for their high ideals and for their cleaving as closely to Scripture as they did. Their mistake was to think that it is the duty of civil government to enforce the first table of the moral law or ten commandments.

To Williams belongs the immortal honour of having been the earliest champion of "soul liberty", as he called it. "I desired," he said of the town of Providence which he founded in Rhode Island, that "it might be a shelter for persons distressed of conscience." This tree survived stormy weather to spread its branches mightily. For instance, American Jews acknowledge with gratitude the liberty afforded them, a liberty uninterrupted since Williams' day. The first Jewish congregation settled in Rhode Island as early as 1658 there to enjoy freedom such as was afforded nowhere else on earth. By 1763 this Jewish congregation had increased to 60 families.

When Williams was banished in 1635 his departure was greatly lamented by his flock at the Church of Salem where he had ministered since 1631.

Without bed or bread for almost four months Williams was the first white man to be cast upon the care of the Indians of that area. God had prepared the way for him in that he had before this time taken the trouble to befriend the Indians, learn their language and preach the Gospel to them. They had come to love him and so took him to themselves in his hour of need. Following this period, Williams set up, together with a few others, a new settlement at Providence, deliberately so named by him because of God's kindness to him during the bitter winter which he described as, "a miserable, cold, howling wilderness" in which he sang his song of pilgrimage as follows:

> God's providence is rich to his,
> Let some distrustful be;
> In wilderness in great distress,
> These ravens have fed me!

The Settlement at Providence was initiated in June 1636, in the territory which soon became known as Rhode Island. In about three years the numbers had increased to about 30 families. In March 1639, Williams and eleven others were baptised and the first Baptist Church in America was constituted.

It is with sadness that we note that those who have enjoyed the clearest apprehensions of truth (including some in our own day) have wavered to become inconsistent in respect of both faith and practice. Williams was in this category. He did not deviate in such a way, however, as to cease enjoying spiritual fellowship with fellow-believers. After founding the Baptist church in Rhode Island he resigned to become a "seeker", a "seeker" being one who despaired of finding a true church by apostolic succession, a strange thing for Baptists to concern themselves with. The root of this error is the notion that it is necessary to trace a line of pure churches right back to apostolic times, which of course it is impossible to do. True believers there have always been but during some periods the churches have been far from pure. Akin to the "seekers" is the error of Old Landmarkism in the Southern States of America today. These people have sought to preserve what they call the "old landmarks". They have assumed that the early Christians were Baptists of their kind and they refuse to acknowledge any other believers or any other kind of ministry as valid.

John Clarke (1609-1676)

Clarke was without question the most eminent Baptist of his time in New England. Certainly he was one of the chief citizens of Rhode Island— politically and religiously.

While scholars argue about the details it can with reasonable certainty be stated that John Clarke formed the second Baptist Church in America at Newport in 1644.

Born in Suffolk, Clarke enjoyed a generous education and practised as a Doctor of Medicine in London for some time. He was also a student of Law which much assisted him when he came to America and aided him when he returned in 1651 with Roger Williams to obtain a charter[1] from the king for Rhode Island. After his arrival, in 1637, he went with a group to New Hampshire but found the climate there too cold, whereupon he turned southwards to Providence where Roger Williams, in typical fashion, gave the group a warm welcome in 1638. Through Williams, Clarke purchased land from the Indians and began a settlement called Newport.

To illustrate the intolerance that existed in the Massachusetts colony it is worth relating the account of a visit made by Clarke and two of his friends, Holmes and Crandall, to a Baptist friend in that colony. While conducting a meeting in the house of a friend whose name was William Witter, the three men were arrested. Clarke was fined £20, Holmes £30 and Crandall £5. On refusal to pay, they were tied to stakes to be whipped but an onlooker was so affected by the sight of Clarke in this condition that he promptly paid the fine on his behalf. Crandall was also rescued but Holmes chose to endure the torture. So powerfully was he sustained while blood poured from his body that he prayed for those who were whipping him and cheerfully declared, "You have struck me with roses". This may well have been a reference, then well known, to a Baptist martyr who suffered under Sir Thomas More. This martyr, James Bainham, a learned barrister, was burned at the stake and when his arms and legs were half consumed he exclaimed in triumph, "Oh ye Papists! behold ye look for miracles, and here you may see a miracle. In this fire I feel no more pain than if I were in a bed of down; it is to me as a bed of roses!" We ought to remember, in the comfort and safety we enjoy today that these early Baptists suffered intensely for their faith and memories of burning and buryings and drownings were fresh upon their minds at that time. In the century previous to that of Clarke it is purported that 30,000 Baptists suffered martyrdom in Holland alone. It was the custom to mock the idea of baptism by bringing about death through drowning or by burial. After laying a body in a coffin a cord was tied around the neck and violently drawn tight whereupon earth was thrown upon the coffin and a living burial made complete. Happily, extreme cruelty was not the custom in Massachusetts. It is to the credit of many of the early American Baptists that they did not bear resentment to their persecutors, which brings us to the story of Henry Dunster.

Henry Dunster (1612-1659)

Dunster was the first President of Harvard College, named after its earliest

---

[1] The remarkable document obtained from Charles II in 1663 was held as fundamental law in Rhode Island until 1842. Included were the words to this effect, "that no person be at any time molested or punished or called in questions for any differences of opinion in matters of religion".

William Gadsby laboured mightily in the north of England being instrumental in establishing about forty churches. Gadsby was a prolific hymn-writer. The hymn book edited and published by him is one of the hall-marks of Gospel Standard Strict and Particular Baptist churches today. Some of his hymns, such as, "Immortal honours rest on Jesus' head", rank with the greatest. Gadsby was a preacher marvellously equipped to reach the working classes. He drew them like a magnet and conversions were frequent. Gadsby tended to be individualistic and unhappily fell into the error of asserting that the Gospel, rather than the moral law, is the rule of life for believers. On the chart (see pages 40-41) it should be added that this is a distinctive tenet of the Gospel Standards. Other Strict Baptists cleave to the 1689 Confession in this matter (cf. ch. 19: sect. 5).

benefactor, the Rev. John Harvard, who dying at the age of 30 left the College half his fortune and a library of about 400 volumes. Henry Dunster, who was born in England and educated at Cambridge where he embraced Puritan principles, came to Boston in 1640. A master of oriental languages he was one of the most learned men of his time and, in establishing Harvard as a centre of learning, he enjoyed outstanding success. He set such a high standard in the liberal arts as to attract students from Bermuda, Virginia and England. Throughout the depression of the 1640's Harvard flourished, the students paying their bills with farm produce. The first printing press in the English colonies and the second in North America was set up at Harvard in 1639. The most amazing achievement of this press was to print the entire Bible in one of the Indian languages, which came about through the initiative of John Eliot. This was the first Bible to be printed in the New World and the first translation into a tribal tongue since Bishop Ulfila turned the Old Testament into Visigothic.

After a thorough and scholarly examination of the question of Baptism, Dunster began to preach against the practice of infant baptism in 1653.

The situation was brought to a head when Dunster refused to have his fourth child sprinkled in 1653. It was after this that he began to make his views known. His views were opposed because believers' baptism struck at the root of the Puritan concept of Church and State. Dunster was indicted on a charge of disturbing worship, for he insisted on airing his views during worship service in a Cambridge church.

He claimed, "that the subjects of baptism were visible, penitent believers, and they only", and also that, "the covenant of Abraham is not a ground of baptism, no, not after the institution thereof. That there were such corruptions stealing into the church, which every faithful Christian ought to bear witness against." This acceptance of Baptist views might have been overlooked had it not been for Dunster's refusal to maintain silence on the matter. For his convictions he paid dearly for after twelve years of brilliant service he was compelled to resign office. In desperate concern for the care of his family during the winter he begged the use of his home for six months until he could settle his affairs. Unhappily this request was rejected. He died only five weeks after moving away from Harvard, but Dunster's example in the midst of his sufferings affords important instruction for us in that he showed a wonderfully magnanimous spirit to his opponents. Cotton Mather says of him that he fell asleep "in such harmony of affection with the good men who had been the authors of his removal from Cambridge, that he by his will ordered his body to be carried there for its burial and bequeathed legacies to these very persons". Inspired by a gracious master we should be generous and large-hearted in all our dealings as was Henry Dunster who, by his firm stand for the truth and by his example planted a seed in the heart of the Puritan Commonwealth of the New World which proved to be indestructible. It ought also to be noted that some of the brightest lights in the Baptist world have come from the opposite camp. Had more love been shown others might have been won, such as a father of American Presbyterianism, namely Archibald Alexander, who for some time refused to baptise infants. He clearly saw the consistent case argued by Baptists who contend not merely for the purity of the ordinance as such, but essentially for the nature of the local church of which believers' baptism is the safeguard.

John Miles (1621-1683)

A brief description of Miles will help illustrate the quality of some of the founding fathers of the Baptist cause in America. Miles was responsible in 1649 for the first Baptist Church in his native land of Wales. He possessed unusual qualities soon to be employed in the New World where he emigrated shortly after the Act of Uniformity in 1662 when 2,000 ministers were ejected from the Established Church. With a large proportion of his church, Miles settled at a new Swansea, about ten miles from Providence in Rhode Island. Despite stout opposition Miles prospered greatly and the new church grew. Once, when brought before the magistrates, he asked for a Bible and quoted Job 19 and verse 28, which reads: "Ye should say, why persecute we him, seeing the root of the matter is found in me?" He said no more but sat down, and the court was so convicted by the context of the passage that cruelty gave way to kindness. Miles was responsible for the establishment of two churches which took deep root in the colony. During these formative years growth was slow and sometimes almost imperceptible, yet these tiny churches grew gradually in size and multiplied in number.

Conclusions

Those Pastors of our day who are labouring in isolated places against great odds should take encouragement. Patience is needed in pioneer work, especially during the times when nothing appears to prosper. The early Baptists faced a hostile world in which they endured persecution. Regarded as sectarian and schismatic, they were often ridiculed, particularly for their adherence to the Scriptural mode of baptism. Being so regarded by the world was hardly an encouragement to evangelise.

These early men have their counterpart today. Difficulties of a different nature militate against Baptist pioneers of the 1970s who are seeking to re-lay solid doctrinal foundations in their churches. They cannot report the sensational results of those who employ modern methods. They are derided as narrow-minded and are accused of division because of their espousal to the old, well-tried doctrines of grace.

Let perseverance be the watchword for these stalwarts who dig deeply in order to build upon a rock stratum. Evangelism is far less difficult today than it was for our forebears even though the church situation seems to have become as intricate as it was in the 17th century. History proves that the Lord will own faithful work and in due season a harvest will be reaped. The Baptist pioneers of America little dreamed that Psalm 72: 16 would find a fulfilment in their case. "There shall be an handful of corn in the earth upon the top of the mountains; the fruit thereof shall shake like Lebanon: and they of the city shall flourish like grass of the earth."

The handful of corn was sown during those early years in adverse conditions and in an environment which seemed in every way to militate against growth. Yet, contrary to human expectation, a harvest of grain was to appear so rich and profuse that it can be compared to a rich harvest of corn, which in the Psalm is likened to the mighty cedars of Lebanon. The reference in the Psalm is to the wind which, when rustling through the ripe ears of corn, would sound similar to the movement of the majestic forests of cedar.

The handful of corn faithfully sown in unpropitious circumstances has enormous potential, for the power of increase belongs to the Lord and this power is clearly seen in spiritual awakenings to which subject we now turn.

2. THE PERIOD OF REVIVALS: 1727-1860

During 1727 a revival took place in the Moravian community in Herrnhut in Germany, and at the same time there was a spiritual awakening under the ministry of Freylinghuysen, a Dutch Reformed minister in New England. When the force of this awakening seemed to be on the decline the Holy Spirit came upon the congregation under Jonathan Edwards at Northampton in 1735, this being one of the most remarkable revivals in the history of the Church. Details of this awakening are recorded in "A Narrative of Surprising Conversions", which Isaac Watts described in this way: "Never did we hear or read since the first ages of Christianity any event of this kind so surprising as the present narrative has set before us." The reading of Edwards' description in the English-speaking world had an incalculable effect in stirring up believers to seek similar blessings. As it happens, this was to be an age of recurring outpourings of the Spirit. It is interesting to note, for instance, that there were at least fifteen major revivals in Wales from 1760 to 1860. Indeed, this was a period during which believers thought in terms of revival. When a spiritual dearth overcame the churches, time would be set aside for fasting and prayer. Re-awakening and the outpouring of the Holy Spirit was earnestly sought. There was no doubt in the minds of these disciples that God was sovereign. He was not obliged, nor could he be forced or compelled to work. His sovereignty in giving grace and salvation was respected. Nevertheless, the believers would implore him to visit them once more and when waited upon with fervency and expectation it often pleased the Lord to come among them to demonstrate the power of his might in salvation.

When it seemed that the impetus of the Edwards awakening was declining, George Whitefield visited America for the second time. His first visit had been confined to Georgia and when he returned to England he experienced the mighty tide of revival, first at Bristol in the open air, and later in London, drawing crowds of an incredible size for those days. These extraordinary happenings are skilfully and accurately portrayed in a fine biography of George Whitefield by Arnold Dallimore. We could well wonder whether after having crossed the Atlantic to America for the second time, if it would please the Lord to use Whitefield in a similar way to that in which he had used him at Moorfields. Our hearts are filled with wonder and praise when we discover that this indeed was to be the case. Whitefield's ministry was used in America to spread the fire from heart to heart, many being quickened in fervent love for the Lord, and multitudes being awakened and retrieved from darkness and brought into the light.

The Baptists benefited greatly from these revivals. Gatherings of considerable magnitude were experienced during this period. An example from the revival which visited the churches in 1800 will illustrate the point. One Association of 29 churches recorded only 29 conversions in 1799. By 1801 the same churches were able to report the reception of over 3,000 members by baptism! In addition to this, nine new churches had been formed during that brief time, and a year later a further ten churches had been formed.[1] One could multiply such instances.

We should avoid the mistake of thinking that these revivals made the work of God a simple matter. Sprague, in his book *Lectures on Revival*,[2] will help correct this erroneous idea. Times of revival are fraught with dangers and difficulties and periods of coldness and unbelief can soon follow, this proving the natural ingratitude and forgetfulness of the human heart.

Short sketches of the lives of some of the leading men of this period will enable us to picture something of the times in which they lived.

John Gano (1727-1798)

A direct descendent of the Huguenots of France, John Gano was born at Hopewell, New Jersey, where he joined the Baptists at a young age. He was ordained in 1754. Before his ordination he was required by the church to give an account of his calling and requested to preach before the members. His calling was immediately recognised and consequently he was sent on a mission to the South. At Charleston he preached before distinguished company, including George Whitefield who was one of twelve ministers present. At first Gano feared this illustrious company but as he began to preach the thought passed through his mind that he had none to fear and obey but the Lord. An idea of his gifts is given

[1] Torbet, *The History of the Baptists*, p. 301.
[2] Banner of Truth.

58

Isaac Backus

by the testimony of an Episcopalian in New York who declared: "Mr. Gano possessed the best pulpit talent of any man that I ever heard." His first pastorate following his itinerant ministry was in New York, where in due course the meeting house had to be enlarged to contain the crowds that flocked to hear him.   In 1763 this church numbered only 41 members.   Gano baptised 297 during his pastorate there.

The revolutionary war interrupted his ministry during which time he distinguished himself as a chaplain in the army.   He showed great courage at the Battle of Chatterton Hill, when he sprang to the front and urged the men to battle when many had fled.   He knew that his rightful place was with the surgeons but confessed that he could not resist the urge to press forward.   The famous men of his day including Washington were among his personal friends.   Gano was noted for his leading role during services of thanksgiving at the end of the war.

Returning to New York, which had been occupied by the English during the war, he and others confronted a scene of desolation.   Of nineteen churches only nine were usable.   Two fires and a plague had swept the city and the work had virtually to begin again.   His own church had been used as a stable by the British.   Gano gathered 37 members of the original 200 and preached his first sermon from Haggai 2: 3, "Who is left among you that saw this house in her first glory?   And how do ye see it now? Is it not in your eyes in comparison of it as nothing?"

With the exception of eight years of service during the war, Gano devoted twenty-six years of his life to his New York pastorate.   In 1787 he moved to Kentucky where he greatly strengthened the Baptist cause.   There had been a powerful revival in Upper Kentucky in 1785.   After a lifetime of distinguished service as a preacher and leader Gano passed to his reward in 1798.

Isaac Backus (1724-1806)

Converted during the Great Awakening, Backus became a Baptist several years later and his life at that stage was typical of the movement toward the Baptist position.   He was involved in the "New Light" controversy. Whitefield's preaching resulted in the division of the Congregationalists into the "New Lights" and "Old Lights" and of the Baptists into the "Separates" and "Regulars" and of the Presbyterians into the "Old Sides" and "New Sides".[1]   The "New Lights", "New Sides" and "Separates" were generally speaking hostile to too much organisation, were more emotional and laid great stress on the necessity of evidence for the conversion experience.   The "New Light" movement tended to consist mostly of the less privileged classes of frontier people in the rural areas.

---

[1] For a lucid description of the religious convictions prior to and during that Awakening under Whitefield see Arnold Dallimore's biography of George Whitefield, pp. 413 ff.

The "Regulars" in contrast, consisted mainly of those in the urban areas who were more conservative and formal in their outlook.

The life of Backus spans a period of much increase among the Baptists. He himself became a foremost Baptist historian, being the author of "A history of New England, with Particular reference to the Baptists"—three volumes, 1777-1796. A powerful preacher, he was by no means confined to the study. The extent of his energies can be gauged by the fact that from 1757-1767 he preached 2,412 sermons while travelling 15,000 miles in New England. In 1740 there were, according to Backus, about 60 Baptist churches and by 1776 this number had increased to 472 and again, by 1795, the number had spiralled to 1,152 churches, representing approximately a twenty-fold increase in 55 years.

Backus is an example of one who used all his talents to the full. He was in every sense an all-rounder, an indefatigable and patient worker which probably accounts for his becoming an able historian. George Bancroft, one of America's favourite authorities on history, said of Backus, "I look always to a Baptist historian for the ingenuousness, clear discernment, and determined accuracy which forms the glory of the great historian Backus." We might add that there is much need for Christians to seek an appreciation of church history and for preachers to encourage a knowledge of the past among their people.

Shubael Stearns

Stearns was a native of Boston. Converted under the preaching of Whitefield he thereafter associated with the "New Lights" (Congregationals). In 1751, however, he became a Baptist and after immersion was ordained as a minister. His fame as a preacher soon spread over a wide area particularly North Carolina. He was instrumental in gathering an immense harvest of souls. Aided by a strong musical voice, his orations were deeply moving often reducing the congregations to tears. One strong opponent of the Baptists, a man by the name of Tidence Lane, who himself afterwards became a distinguished Baptist minister, confessed that he could not resist the urge to go and hear Mr. Stearns despite his loathing of Baptists. The preaching was so used that day that Lane, despite all the power of his will to resist, was unable to stand upright upon his feet, but sank to the ground under overwhelming conviction of sin.

Although limited in education, Stearns possessed much discernment and was responsible for the establishment of the well-known church at Sandy Creak in North Carolina. From this base, 42 other local churches were formed. Stearns is included in this outline of brief biographies because he was typical of the times. Stearns worked with his brother-in-law, Daniel Marshall, and Col. Samuel Harriss, a trio which co-operated as well in their way as did the famous Carey, Marshman and Ward in India. These three constituted the main leadership of the Separate Baptists in

Richard Fuller

the U.S.A. Marshall was an ex-Presbyterian minister who had been a missionary to the Mohawk Indians.

Other men of the same calibre characterised this period, such as Hezekiah Smith who attended the first Baptist school in America (Hopewell Academy in New Jersey—1756). He graduated from Princeton in 1762. He is credited with the founding of thirteen churches.

Richard Fuller (1804-1876)

Fuller graduated from Harvard College at the head of his class in 1824. He then studied law and rose to eminence in his profession. It is sometimes pointed out today that when some folk cannot succeed at anything else they try the ministry. Not so with Richard Fuller. He left a very lucrative practice a year after his conversion which took place in 1831. When Christ was revealed to him he was so affected that he said, "My soul ran over with love and joy and praise: for days I could not eat or sleep." The first church of which he was the minister was feeble initially, but he was used to build it up to 200 European members and 2,400 Black. He sometimes spent weeks away from home, preaching day after day in the South. In 1847 he became pastor of a Baptist church in Baltimore. There were 87 members at the time but the membership grew to 1,200 under his ministry.

Richard Fuller was typical of several preachers of the period in placing great stress on the authority of Scripture and in emphasising a close walk with Christ. He was essentially a worker combining much study with pastoral visitation. When he preached it was as though he had come direct from the presence of God. He was a proclaimer of the Gospel who was appreciated in many parts of the nation.

Stephen Gano (1762-1828)

Gano's early years as a ship's surgeon were hazardous. On several occasions he narrowly escaped with his life. Eventually however he entered medical practice which terminated when he was set aside to the ministry of the Gospel. How mightily the Holy Spirit was working during those times, in comparison with the spiritual dearth that has come upon us during the 20th century, can be seen when we survey some of the details of the fruitfulness of men like Stephen Gano.

For instance, in 1792 he became pastor of the First Baptist Church at Providence where he was to minister until his death 36 years later. When he came to Providence there were 165 members in the church. At the time of his death the number had risen to 648. But that is not the end of the story. This church had had five children in the form of five other churches. Gano's labours were not confined to this sphere of home church and home mission work. He had an executive ability which he employed on behalf of the Association of Baptist churches and for nineteen years he acted as moderator. This was a time of revivals and several times his church was visited with outpourings of the Holy Spirit. Would to God that we could experience revivals again. In those days revivals were recognised for what they are—spontaneous visitations from God which arise entirely out of his sovereign mercy. Alas, today many think that revivals can be arranged or organised. Gano baptised hundreds of converts, including his six daughters, four of whom married Baptist ministers.

Gano knew many personal heartaches, losing three wives by death. He was an invalid for his last few years on earth. Still he continued to preach until three months before death.

John Leland (1754-1841)

It is not possible to mention all the worthies of this period and undoubtedly, criticism can be made of any man's choice. The purpose here is to introduce some of the leaders of the past and give some idea of the extent of their achievements through the gracious enablement of God.

Leland spent much of his life in travel but fifteen years were spent as pastor of a church in Virginia. Here he baptised 700 persons. The statistics that have been given in sketching these thumbnail biographies could be misleading if we compared them with some figures reported today. Conversion meant more in those days. Salvation was not presented as a result of following an easy formula. Take Gano's own conversion for instance. It came after the most intense agonies of soul. His sins convicted him to the point of torment and hell opened up before him. Bunyan's conviction of sin was similar. It is not to be assumed that all these men were orthodox Calvinists in their beliefs about salvation. Leland claimed to be a Calvinist and was well aware of the difference between Gill, Fuller and Wesley. He struggled in his mind as to the best way of addressing sinners and leading them to repentance.

John Leland believed strongly in a free society where people should be allowed to speak and worship as they please. This was fine in itself but it may have led Leland to oppose the idea of Confessions of Faith. Unwittingly he contributed to the decline in doctrinal standards which was to come and he is an example of a gifted man whose unbalanced attitude contributed to the weakening of the churches at a later period.

Adoniram Judson (1788-1850) and Luther Rice (1782-?)

These two men emerged from a revivalistic atmosphere which fostered zealous missionary concern. It is to the credit of the Baptists that they had given generous financial support to the Congregational Mission Board which was responsible for sending Judson and Rice to India. Independently of each other, while crossing the high seas, these two men came to see the Scriptural nature of baptism by immersion. This involved

64

Arthur W. Pink is regarded as the most prolific free grace writer this century. The above photo of Mr. Pink and his wife was taken in Australia in the 1920s. The details of his ministry illustrate some of the tensions experienced among Baptists this century. A biographical study of his early life is included in "Reformation Today" No. 11. The magazine is available from Carey Publications.

them in a terrible dilemma. No alternative existed but that of resignation from the Board, whereupon the Baptists welcomed them into their family. Luther Rice returned to the States and became to the cause of Baptist overseas missions what Andrew Fuller was to Carey and his colleagues in India. He travelled from Boston throughout the Middle and Southern States. His work resulted in a Convention in Philadelphia in 1814, from which a Society was established called "The Baptist General Convention for Foreign Missions". (It was also called the "Triennial Convention" since it met every three years.) The Judsons were adopted as the first missionaries. In the meantime they had been driven by the intolerance of the Government of Bengal to Rangoon. The measure of Adoniram's tenacity can be gauged by the fact that despite the most appalling difficulties he was able to lay the whole Bible, faithfully translated, before the Burmese people twenty-one years later. This is wonderful when we consider the responsibilities which he bore, together with the fact that he spent agonising years in prison, during which time he was as near to facing a violent death as was Daniel when he was thrown into the lions' den. The courage of Ann Judson under intense privation is one of the most inspiring examples of perseverance in the annals of the Church.

Initially the mission to the Burmese was as tedious in its progress as was Carey's work in its commencement. When the British Government took over Burma, a copious hinterland of gospel opportunity opened up by way of preaching to the Karens who were a people of the hills and forests. Glorious gains were made, 30,000 being baptised in 1886. Only about 1,200 Burmese were converted in the same period.

The influence of Judson and Rice in creating interest in missionary work can hardly be over-estimated. Judson continually prompted the churches at home to broaden their enterprise to include Thailand, Indo-China, China and Japan. Rice, at 31 years of age in 1813, was already arresting the attention of many congregations, using his great ability as a speaker to quicken zeal for missions. He was a prime mover in enlisting support, not only for overseas work but also in the sending out of the first missionaries to the American West. John Mason Peck and James E. Welsh were the first home missionaries sent out to the West in 1817. Peck himself becoming an enthusiast in creating new interest in evangelising the expanding western frontiers. It should be noted that Luther Rice early saw the necessity for a well-trained ministry if overseas missions were to be successful.

3. THE AGE OF HUMAN ORGANISATION: 1860-1976

These biographical sketches illustrate that revivals were instrumental in bringing about the great missionary awakening. To meet the needs of the day it is understandable that a tremendous emphasis should be laid on missionary activity. Growing Associations vied with each other in the evangelisation of new fields. Of these Associations the American

Baptist Convention led the way at the beginning but, in due course, the Southern Baptist Convention was to outgrow the Northern counterpart by six or seven times. As the years went on, a new force of liberalism emerged which had to be combatted and this did much to enervate the work of evangelicals. Baptists suffered, as did other bodies, by the growth of higher criticism which undermined faith in the Scriptures. The decline in doctrinal standards was largely responsible for the advance of unbelief which began to harass some of the Associations. This brought division and separation in some of the missionary societies.

It is difficult to choose leading figures from this period. There were many men of vision, some of whom possessed a genius for organisation. This gift was needed in order to contend with the increasing needs of expanding frontiers. Impressive statistics illustrating growth and vivid descriptions of expansion are not hard to find. The Baptists were industrious in the establishment of seminaries, training schools, academies and colleges. Many of these, however, were soon to fall into the disastrous error of regarding the Scriptures as merely human documents.

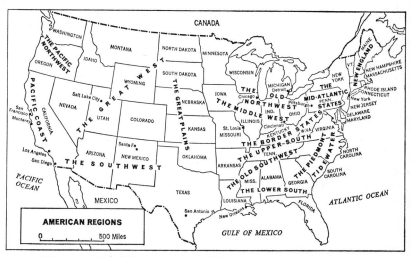

This map is included as a reminder of the enormous size of the country.
It will also help readers locate the different States.

We come now to an analysis of this period, which is designated "the period of human organisation" because of the beliefs that have come to prevail in Baptist circles concerning both God and man. As we do so, we remember the statistics mentioned at the beginning and remind ourselves that in 1960 the Southern Baptist Convention claimed a membership of about 9,700,000 while the Northern Baptist Convention numbered about 1,500,000. The National Baptist Convention, representing the negro population, numbered an astonishing 7,500,000. The Regular Baptist churches, which trace their history back to the Great Awakening, being the conservative side as explained just now, numbered 135,000. There

John Leland

are innumerable smaller bodies, including foreign-speaking groups such as the Danish, Hungarian and Italian Baptist Associations.

Naturally, the dates used to demarcate these sections are arbitrary. It would be wrong to conclude that revivals ceased altogether after 1858-60. For instance, an account has been written describing the revivals experienced in the camps of the Confederate armies during the Civil War of 1862-1865[1]. Multitudes were added to the churches in the South between 1872 and 1880.

Application

The outstanding question to emerge from our survey is: why have revivals disappeared? Organised religion has more and more come to predominate in the minds of evangelicals, with the result that now there is confusion as to what revival really is. It is not uncommon in America today for revivals to be announced before the time! In the minds of the majority of Baptists in America organised crusades and revivals are synonymous. This, of course, is far removed from the biblical concept of the outpouring of the Holy Spirit. A definition of revival from Scripture can be found in the second chapter of Acts, in the 17th verse Peter quotes the prophet Joel—"I will pour out of my Spirit". These words show clearly that both in regard to timing and locality the outpouring of the Spirit belongs entirely to God. It is his sole prerogative to pour out his Spirit. Indeed it can be said that nothing militates more against genuine revival than the presumption that we can control God.

The predominance of humanly organised, decisionist Christianity has resulted in self-deception which is widespread. The idea that people can receive Christ as Saviour and yet not as Lord and Master prevails in many quarters. We are reminded of our Lord's solemn words: *"Every plant, which my heavenly Father hath not planted, shall be rooted up"* Matt. 15: 13. We have become accustomed to using the word "Arminian" to describe those who believe in the free will of man and who reject the idea that man's will is enslaved by sin. We do not think carefully enough about some of these terms. Perhaps the following definitions will help:

The Pelagian believes that anyone who wills to become a Christian can do so.

The semi-Pelagian believes that God's help is necessary for a man to become a Christian.

The Arminian believes that God gives equal ability to all and that some men use this ability to become Christians and some do not.

The Lutheran believes that without God's prevailing grace men will not believe. Those who resist this grace are lost while those who do not resist are saved.

[1] John W. Jones, Atlanta, 1904.

The Calvinist believes that men by nature will never believe and that God's regeneration is essential, this quickening being the cause of repentance and faith.

But this list is not adequate. We need to make room for a new class as will be illustrated presently, namely:

The Xavierite believes that anyone who responds to an appeal is, and should be, recognised as a Christian.

Francis Xavier (1506-1552) was a disciple of Ignatius Loyola, founder of the Jesuits. Few men in history can compare with Xavier for zeal. There is a false zeal such as that which characterises Communists and Jehovah's Witnesses and a mixed zeal in which truth is mixed with error. It is hard to say how much truth there was with Xavier. He was prodigious in his efforts to evangelise, pioneering in both India and Japan. In South India whole village populations were baptised. To Xavier, assent to Christianity was adequate. If whole communities embraced the Christian name then whole communities were sprinkled.

The idea is widespread in America that the mere acceptance of Christ as saviour ensures salvation. Acceptance of Christ as Lord can follow later. Even when lives are destitute of evidence of a saving change they are still regarded as Christian, on the grounds of a decision once made. Such "fruitless" professors are termed "carnal Christians".

It cannot be denied that the profession of faith which is required today is of a very shallow kind. The kind of evangelism prevailing today, particularly as propagated by such as the Southern Baptist Convention, is a type of Xavierism. They baptise large numbers upon profession of faith but, instead of sprinkling like Xavier, they immerse those who have given assent to Christ. But, profession of faith does not regenerate. John the Baptist said, "A man can receive nothing except it be given him from above." Regeneration is from heaven and is not something we can control. It is our task to preach and spread the word. It is God's prerogative to regenerate.

Dr. C. E. Autrey, leading Southern Baptist spokesman, puts it this way:

Lead people to pray . . . create a deep spiritual concern . . . promote complete surrender . . . organisational preparation is vital. . . . Publicity is also essential for all types of revival meetings. It creates expectancy. It advertises the great spiritual values of the crusade. . . . Evangelistic singing is an essential part in revival. . . . A stirring song service brightens the atmosphere and assimilates the motley crowd into a congregation of worshippers.

Three things will help assure big attendance and phenomenal results. They are: 1. Organisation; 2. Involvement; 3. Proper Publicity.

He follows this explanation by saying that between 1954 and 1964 the Southern Baptists won to Christ and baptised 4,334,000. The same writer explains how this can be done in other countries as though it were all a simple matter of method.

These statements by C. E. Autrey were made at the World Congress for Evangelism held in Berlin in 1966. They typify the outlook of many. Exaggerated reports in magazines reflect this. For instance a headline in *The South African Baptist* stated that there had been 708 converts in a crusade in Dallas. In reading the report, however, we are told that there were 708 professions of faith. Converts and professions of faith are not the same thing, but this very superficial kind of exaggeration passes in most Baptist magazines. How did Xavierism come to prevail on such a wide scale? Why is it that so many today are victims of Xavierism?

We have to go back to the time of Charles G. Finney for the answer. Finney exercised a profound influence, not only in his own denomination but upon evangelicals everywhere. If you read his lectures on *Revivals of Religion* you will find that he teaches that revival can be produced whenever we really want to produce it. He declares: "A revival is nothing else than a new beginning of obedience to God."[1]

Finney was quite dogmatic about the fact that a revival is a natural thing. It is not a miracle, nor dependent on a miracle, in any sense. It is purely the outcome of the right use of the constituted means—as much so as any other effect is produced by the application of means.[2] In other words, Finney propounded the view that revival could be produced at any time. Finney also laid stress on the "anxious seat", that is calling people to the front. This technique encouraged the call for decisions which is a major feature of evangelistic crusades today. In addition to this, Finney also stressed the need for novelty, that is that we should always be ready to abandon old methods and invent new ones to attract and hold the attention of the people, and bring them by moral persuasion to make the necessary decision. Finney made no bones about the fact that he believed that "religion is the work of man. It is something for man to do. It consists in obeying God. It is man's duty." This stress on human ability has paved the way to the situation which prevails almost everywhere today. But we should also investigate why there has been so little opposition to this kind of religion in which it is supposed that men can use and control God as though he were a slot-machine.

As early as 1707 the Philadelphia Baptist Association was formed, which was destined to have an extensive influence upon Baptists in America throughout the years. In 1742 this Association authorised the publication of the *London Confession of Particular Baptists of 1689*, the same statement of faith which was re-published by Spurgeon in his opening years at New Park Street in London. It has been the most popular confession for Reformed Baptists since the Puritan era. The Philadelphia Association was instrumental in winning much ground for the Reformed faith. Men of the Philadelphia Association were missionary-minded and, generally speaking, leaders in education and in progressive ideas. However, during

[1] *Revivals of Religion—1840*, p. 8.

[2] Ibid., p. 5.

Adoniram Judson

the 19th century the position of this Association weakened and apart from the publication of the *New Hampshire Confession of Faith*, which was drawn up in 1830 to offset Arminian teaching in New England, there was relatively little to stem the tidal wave of decisionist Christianity.

In addition to this, the Reformed cause was much weakened by false Calvinism in the form of the peculiar "Two Seed in the Spirit" denomination which, at one stage, had 13,000 members but which has now only about 200. There was also the primitive "Anti-Mission Baptists" who numbered over 120,000 in 1844. They have declined to about 65,000 members today. The charge is constantly reiterated that the Reformed are anti-missionary and anti-evangelistic. The presence of hyper-Calvinism in different forms has done much to discredit the true Reformed witness.

The greatest need for Baptists is to return in faith and practice to the truths of Scripture. These truths are capable of definition. If we are not prepared to contend for intelligible truth then we are in no position to resist the forces of Liberalism and Ecumenism. Our evangelistic methods will continue to be superficial, effeminate and even ludicrous unless we recognise the necessity of worthy biblical exposition and the need to honour the sovereignty of the Holy Spirit. Much more analytical thinking is required that we might with more compassion and insight address the peculiar problems of our age. Francis Schaeffer's contribution is noteworthy in this respect.

Superficiality is a disease that has invaded every area of life. Indeed, this is not true of the Baptists alone. A. W. Tozer put it this way:

Evangelical Christianity, at least in the United States, is now tragically below the New Testament standard. Worldliness is an accepted part of our way of life. Our religious mood is social instead of spiritual. We have lost the art of worship.

We are not producing saints. Our models are successful businessmen, celebrated athletes and theatrical personalities. We carry on our religious activities after the methods of the modern advertiser. Our homes have been turned into theatres. Our literature is shallow and our hymnody borders on sacrilege. And scarcely anyone appears to care.

The widespread, increasing stress on human activity has resulted in a proliferation of human organisations and societies, with the result that we have largely lost sight of the fact that God has commissioned only one form of organisation which is the local church. We should seek, therefore, to establish strong local churches in which there is comprehensive teaching along the lines of systematic, expository preaching.

Evangelism which stems from the local church, upon a long-term basis, including oversight and discipline of those members who engage in this form of work, is what we should aim at. While we continue to strive for a return to the biblical pattern in regard to local churches we should, at the same time, seek a revival from heaven. We should not lose sight of the fact that God has not changed and while our ever-present duty is the reformation of the church as well as fervent evangelism and missionary outreach, it is God's prerogative to send awakening.

This long-term approach may seem unexciting and unsensational to evangelicals who have been fed with milk and misled by organisations, but I am persuaded that non-church-based activities which have abandoned the local church have been to the detriment of the cause of God over the last 100 years, despite all their claims to magnificent results. The evidence points to the fact that there has been an actual decline in spirituality and in genuine conversion work while all these fantastic claims have been made concerning success in organised crusades.

But as we seek to do what we can, we remember that revivals are a reality. Surely this study reminds us that the first need in the United States and the whole world today is Revival—an outpouring of the Spirit of God in convicting men of their sin and bringing them into the new life of union with the Lord Jesus Christ. Revival has a twin sister, Reformation— reformation of the doctrine and structure of the church. The only doctrine of the Bible regarding salvation is Reformed doctrine, and the only doctrine regarding the nature of the church is Baptist, *gathered church* doctrine. In seeking to establish Reformed, Baptist churches, we are working in accordance with the will of God as revealed in his Word. It is, of course, possible for such churches to be orthodox and lifeless, but this in no way lessens the fact that Reformed theology and believers' baptism are alone scriptural.

Although such a large percentage of Baptist churches has failed because of wrong theology, the principle of the gathered church, the only gateway to which is regeneration with its sign of baptism, is none the less the teaching of the New Testament. The Reformers of the 16th century recovered the doctrine of justification by faith, and tremendous blessing to the world was the result; but they failed to recover the doctrine of the gathered church. We have seen subsequently that it is as easy to be an unregenerate Protestant as an unregenerate Roman Catholic.

History is "his story"—the story of God at work in the world fulfilling his predestined, infallible purposes. He is at work in grace—in calling sinners out of the world to form his Church—and in judgment, declaring his holiness in his wrath against all forms of ungodliness. In tracing the history of the Baptist movement in America we have seen the triumphs of his grace, but we have had also to map out the more recent roadway, a downward way of declension into superficiality and neglect and rejection of truth. As we see so much that is dishonouring to God let us heed the Lord's command to Jeremiah, "Call unto me, and I will answer thee, and shew thee great and mighty things, which thou knowest not" Jer. 33: 3.

BIBLIOGRAPHY

Those who relish history will find Admiral Morison's, *History of the American People*, 1,150 pp., O.U.P., a source of enjoyment and relaxation. For the general reader this is the ideal volume. Wide in its sweep it nevertheless contains adequate detail, being interspersed with the author's interpretations, particularly with regard to the analysis of personalities, war strategies and political events. As is common with secular authors, Morison is neither discerning nor accurate with regard to the Gospel. For instance, he attributes too much to Jonathan Edwards: "Edwards' preaching at Northampton was the womb of all modern revivalism", p. 152. John R. Alden's *Pioneer America*, Hutchinson, 310 pp., and *History of the American Revolution*, 541 pp., are also highly readable and full of well documented material.

The History of the Baptists, by Thomas Armitage, 977 pp., last published in 1887, contains a mine of information presented in a colourful style. If you come across a copy procure it if you can. After this I consulted Torbet, Vedder and Maring. A contemporary Baptist, Edward H. Overby, has written *A Short History of the Baptists*, 148 pp., Independent Baptist Publications, 8321 Ballard Road, Niles 48, Illinois. No price is shown. The same author, together with N. B. Magruder, is responsible for an informative article on Baptists in *The Encyclopaedia of Christianity*. As we would expect the Baptist Union Library, Southampton Row, London, possesses a wide range of books on Baptist history, but I searched in vain for adequate material on America. Other libraries were consulted but it was not until a visit to Bucknell University, Lewisburg, Pennsylvania, that pure gold was discovered and lots of it! Lining the shelves at Bucknell are volumes recording detailed histories of the different Associations from Maine and Vermont in the North-East right across the country. Using these sources it is possible for instance to extract details as to the character and extent of particular revivals such as that of 1800-1801.

The map on page 67 is included by permission of Hutchinson the Publishers.

Georgi Vins

BAPTISTS IN RUSSIA TODAY

A T the Olympic Games at Montreal in 1976 over six thousand athletes strove to win medals which with the process of time will tarnish.   In another arena incorruptible crowns are being won.   In this, the spiritual stadium, Russian believers are undoubtedly to the fore.   Those who seek examples of apostolic Christianity in the twentieth century will find much to encourage them in Russia.   The testimony of the Baptists in particular provides a source of inspiration.   This does not overlook the example of Christians in other lands dominated by Communism.   Conditions pertaining in countries such as East Germany, Poland and Rumania are discussed briefly in the chapter surveying the position of Baptists throughout the world.

With regard to countries dominated by atheistic Communism it is not easy to obtain reliable information.   Efforts to annihilate Christianity in China, North Vietnam, North Korea and Albania have been severe in the extreme.   Conditions differ widely even from area to area inside countries such as Bulgaria and Rumania, to cite two examples, and the same applies to the Soviet Union.

When considering Russia, which is so important because of its size and leadership in the Communist world, detailed information is available. Much of this has been provided because of the foresight and courage of those who love the Gospel in that land.

Accounts of court trials and imprisonments are reported in most free countries.   Russian writers, the Jews and the Baptists have been the centre of interest in their struggles for freedom and these groups have provided information.[1]

Solzhenitsyn is the best known of contemporary Russian writers.   He has a brilliant gift of exposing the emptiness of materialism and the tragic consequences of revolution for revolution's sake.   He mourns the loss of a whole generation of Russian writers who have been buried in prison camps.[2]   That he himself has survived a long ordeal under such conditions is amazing.   During 1976 Solzhenitsyn stirred all Britain in a television interview.   His work *Gulag Archipelago* in three volumes describing the mammoth Soviet liquidation programme (on a par with Hitler's machine) is being widely read in English.   All religious minorities have suffered in Russia, the Jews in particular.

But our purpose is to consider the Baptists in Russia today and in doing this it will be essential to view their origins and history.   First it will help to refer to one of the difficulties which confronts us with this subject. That is the appearance of liberty that is intentionally given by the Communist regime in Russia.

This policy can be illustrated by a large Baptist church which is permitted to function freely in Moscow.   Distinguished visitors from the West (including President Nixon during 1972) are much impressed by the large, fervent congregation, this assembly prospering to the extent of five thousand members and six services every week.   Religious reporters display enthusiasm in their descriptions of this church, which is very much to the advantage of the Communist hierarchy.   A tough policy for practising Christians exists behind this facade of religious toleration.   For instance an article in the *Baptist Times*[3] gives a glowing account of freedom for personal evangelism.   Nothing could be further from the truth. While naive readers absorb this deception, not a few believers are being subjected to torture and death in Soviet prisons.   Some of these martyrs are pastors and leaders of unusual calibre.   Their lives are an inspiration. Those who may be alive still should be the constant subject of our prayers as should their wives and children.

The official total of Baptists in the Soviet Union is 550,000.   This represents a denomination which is governed by Communist officialdom.   The Moscow showpiece already referred to, which is reputed to have fourteen daughter churches, forms part of it.   This official denomination is infiltrated and to a large extent is subservient to the State.   It is difficult to judge numbers but those who devote their time to research in this subject believe that the official or registered Baptist denomination is considerably smaller than its advertised size.   On the other hand those Baptists who have refused to submit to State control, known as the unregistered Baptists, could possibly number more than three million. These carry on as best they can without the liberties of property, buildings, new Bibles, books, magazines and printing—liberties that we would find it difficult to do without.   It is from this courageous, uncompromising body that about six hundred people have been taken and held at various times under severe conditions since 1960, with never less than one hundred and fifty in prison at any one time.[4]   It should not be imagined that the State-recognised Baptists are not themselves subject to persecution; it would be grossly unfair to oversimplify their position, especially since their witness is often just as heroic as that of unrecognised groups.   Their advantages are few: the right to have a correspondence course with about a hundred students enrolled and permission for seven students to study in other countries—just enough to give the appearance of freedom. Many genuine and sincere Christians maintain a very faithful witness within the State-controlled Baptist denomination (known as the A.U.C.E.C.B., to be explained in more detail presently).

Baptist Origins in Russia 1867-1917

In Revelation 13 two hideous beasts are described. These rise out of the sea and are generally taken to represent anti-Christian government and anti-Christian religion. Both beasts have breathed their horrors upon Russia and particularly the former has been given not only to blaspheme God, but also to war against and wear down the Soviet saints. To these believers has belonged a baptism of suffering, generation after generation.

Before the Reformation the Christian religion in Western Europe was Roman Catholic and monolithic in form, while that in Eastern Europe was Greek Orthodox and likewise monolithic in character. The Reformation won some countries to Protestantism and as we saw in English Baptist history, very soon there were dissenting or non-conformist groups or denominations within Protestantism. In Russia the monolithic structure of religious orthodoxy was to carry on unchallenged for much longer. Protestant religion was eventually to arrive from other parts of Europe. German immigrants, but also Englishmen, as well as Lutherans from Latvia and Estonia helped to foster indigenous evangelical growth. The Gospels were published in the vernacular in 1819 which indicates some of the earliest efforts to evangelise.

In 1867 Nikita Voronin was immersed in a river in the Caucasus, thus marking the beginning of the Baptist cause which soon began to grow, assisted by the capable and resilient leadership of men such as Ivanov and Pavlov.

Two other independent areas of Baptist growth were the Ukraine and Leningrad. Johann Oncken the gifted German leader referred to in the introduction, carried out missionary work in the Ukraine. There had been a revival in the 1850s among the *Stundists* (*Stunde* meaning "hour" referred to their time of prayer and Bible study). Oncken well understood the significance and necessity of local churches and his work to achieve the establishment of such was successful.

The Leningrad work owed much to the famous Lord Radstock, a Plymouth Brother (Open Brethren) who moved in aristocratic circles in Russia. Hundreds of ordinary people gathered to hear the Gospel preached in the lavish homes of these wealthy Russian nobles. A remarkable evangelical awakening took place.

Soon these various groups situated in the Caucasus, Ukraine and Leningrad began to encourage each other and in 1884 a conference was convened

Johann Oncken (1800-1884) pastor of the first Baptist church in Hamburg, began to preach at the age of 24 and became a Baptist at 34 when the church of which he was pastor was founded. Oncken and his associates pioneered in the planting of churches in several countries in Europe. When the growth of the church in Hamburg necessitated a new building in 1867 C. H. Spurgeon was one of the preachers at the opening services. Let us pray for men of Oncken's and Spurgeon's church-planting vision and zeal to be raised up to meet the needs for the harvest fields of today.

with the aim of uniting the evangelicals. This proved premature but it is clear that a footing had been gained in a country which was as formally committed to Eastern Orthodoxy with its incense, smoking candles and icons as Spain is today to Mary, the Saints and the Confessional.

Early rumbles of persecution came as a presage of what, with little respite, was to characterise the country throughout the course of the next century. Pavlov for instance recorded his experience (*Memoirs of an Exile*) and describes his arrest and imprisonment in 1891. In exile, hunger and privation joined hands to bring about the death of Pavlov's wife and four children, leaving Pavlov only one son. One other daughter had died in a drowning accident. Pavlov was comforted by believers who travelled long distances for fellowship with him to strengthen his faith after his agonising bereavement.

Despite repressions by the Tsarist regime the Baptists grew rapidly during the first decade of this century.

1917-1976

The coming to power of a new government in March 1917 brought much relief to the evangelical cause. Religious restrictions were abolished and freedom declared for those imprisoned for religious offences. Exiled and imprisoned Baptists returned home. This opportunity was well utilised and it is said that never was there more biblical, evangelical preaching in Russia than there was during that year. Since Lenin legislated freedom of religion for all citizens, the coming to power in 1917 of the Communist Party was much to the advantage of the Baptists. Despite persecution from the Russian Orthodox Church they were to enjoy their best decade as far as freedom was concerned. Bibles were printed and literature work increased.

Stalin succeeded Lenin in 1924. He followed the policy of totalitarianism to the utmost limit. The notorious Stalinist purges inflicted gaping wounds upon Soviet Society as a whole, and it was not only the Baptists who suffered. Laws were enacted in 1929 which were to enchain and hamper believers as never before. Teaching of religion to anyone under eighteen was forbidden. Further legislation was enacted enforcing atheistic teaching in all schools, no parent being allowed to contract his child out of this teaching. The author has personally witnessed the effects of this, not in Russia but in Eastern Europe, and can testify that this is an agonising experience for evangelical parents. It is by no means easy for them to counteract the anti-Christian propaganda to which their children are constantly subjected.

Further restrictions concern gatherings. These are forbidden unless permission is obtained. Not only buildings but pastors have to be registered. This registration, if and when it does work, ensures that the church rests in the great iron paw of the State. The same policy of

81

allowing such a small fraction of freedom as to give the appearance of liberty, but at the same time stifling Christian influence, applies to literature. Conditions went from bad to worse under Stalin and during the 1930s leading Baptists were imprisoned. The most famous of these was Nikolai Odinstov. Arrested in 1933, he was eaten alive six years later, dogs having been set upon him by his keepers. This was typical of the nightmare experienced under Stalin.

During the war the government set up a commission by which to gain supreme authority over the church. To bring all evangelicals together the A.U.C.E.C.B. (All Union Council of Evangelical Christians and Baptists) was created by the State. These letters A.U.C.E.C.B. are very important and the religious situation in Russia cannot be rightly comprehended unless the origin, nature and function of the A.U.C.E.C.B. is grasped. The secret police by infiltrating the churches obtained files of personal information which enabled them to place non-evangelical leaders (or those who were ready to compromise) over the A.U.C.E.C.B. At the same time men of robust conviction were marked out as the real sources of evangelical power and influence.

Just as a man controls a concertina so State officials were able, and are still able, to increase or diminish restrictions. Those who compromise with them become religious pawns playing their game. By granting some privileges the officials sometimes deceive believers and cause them to think that a new and better epoch may be on the way. At the time of the formation of the A.U.C.E.C.B. advantage was taken of the weak physical state of those returning from Siberia. After a gruelling ordeal these victims had little physical strength.

The Devil has exploited the position by fanning the flames of resentment in those who refuse to have anything to do with the A.U.C.E.C.B. Just as those who come out of major apostate denominations in the West can be tempted to be bitter about those who remain within, so is there this tension in the Russian situation. Love is the duty of all believers and nothing is gained by strife.

Nevertheless it is difficult not to feel strongly about neglect of the persecuted. For instance in May 1971 the *Evangelical Times* exposed the A.U.C.E.C.B. by publishing a letter addressed to Dr. Talbert, President of the *Baptist World Alliance*. This letter came from the Second Conference of the Relatives of Prisoners from the Churches of Evangelical Christian Baptists. Dr. Talbert had visited the government shop window of religious freedom. He had been received by the Kremlin but ignored the plight of those who had suffered or been imprisoned for their faith in Christ. He did not visit any persecuted church. The letter aptly quoted the text, "Sick and in the shadow of death and ye visited me not".

In 1960 the A.U.C.E.C.B. published a revised set of statutes to replace those set up at its inauguration in 1944. The new statutes reveal the radical determination of the Communists to repress and ultimately destroy biblical religion, this purpose lying behind an outward appearance of plutocracy as though the body exists for the wellbeing of everybody. One of the effects of the new statutes was to strengthen large numbers of Baptists and other evangelical groups which had never been in the A.U.C.E.C.B. and also arouse determined opposition to the official Baptist leadership of the A.U.C.E.C.B.

The new statutes proved to be an all-out Communist attack upon Christianity. Krushchev was endeavouring to strengthen the Communist Party. He desired to build up his ideological forces. Like Nero before him he found in the Christian church an ideal whipping boy upon which could be unleashed a timely and advantageous deluge of persecution. The full force of this was to last from 1960-1964. But despite the exit of Krushchev in 1964 repression and imprisonment continue to this day.

Having outlined some lives of foremost Baptist leaders of past generations it is fitting that a sketch be provided of at least one Baptist hero of our day. In a sense the choice is arbitrary since it depends upon information to hand. Many other lives could be described but the testimony of this one can illustrate well the situation prevailing in Russia today.

Georgi Vins

Born in 1924, Georgi was to have his father for only three years, Peter Vins being callously taken away to a prison camp in 1927 where he died two years later. This was especially tragic since Georgi's father possessed knowledge very unusual for a Russian. He had studied in America and was an accomplished and devoted scholar. These valuable gifts were denied to the church and to his son. However, his mother helped fill the gap. She managed to procure a good education for Georgi, nurturing in him the convictions of her husband, whose life had so soon been removed from her. The State persecutes the families of bereaved Christians. The efforts of Georgi's mother to equip him are to be the more admired on this account.

His father having perished as a result of the Stalinist purge, Georgi was in turn to find himself in the teeth of Krushchev's campaign against the godly. Alienated by the compromise of men enmeshed in the A.U.C.E.C.B. Georgi contributed toward the leadership of the Reform Baptists. The latter standing outside the A.U.C.E.C.B. are known as Reform Baptists or unregistered Baptists. Their leadership is sometimes referred to as "The Action Group".

An able poet and author, Georgi wrote articles of immense value for believers. He concentrated in particular upon exposition of those Scriptures which refer to the duty of Christians to nurture their children and families, and he explained the practicalities of this under conditions which are intensely hostile to the truth. He and a fellow leader Kryuchkov were tried in 1966 for publishing literature and distributing it widely. The method employed in this trial was to bring the accused to a condition of physical exhaustion. Nevertheless in his final defence Vins delivered verses full of truth, two of which we quote even though the eloquence is lost through translation.

> Forgetful of history's lessons,
> They burn with desire to punish
> Freedom of conscience and of faith
> And the right to serve the Lord.

> No! You cannot kill the freedom of belief,
> Or imprison Christ in jail!
> The examples of His triumphs
> Will live in hearts He's saved.

Vins was sentenced to three years in a "special regime" camp. His mother, Lidia, a highly qualified language translator earning a substantial salary, was forbidden to continue in her profession since punishment applies also to the family of an offender. Lidia Vins and other women whose relatives had been imprisoned have compiled records describing and documenting the situation in Russia. When analysed, these reveal that the majority of those prepared to suffer for their faith are not just old people of a past religious era, but young people who have grown up under Communism and who have been subjected to the full force of atheistic propaganda.

Georgi Vins almost succumbed during three years of imprisonment. Although a qualified engineer he was compelled to work as a beast of burden which included walking to and from the place of labour six miles away. Appeals for him to be employed as an electrician at the camp were ignored by the authorities who seemed determined to bring about his liquidation.

In January 1975 Georgi Vins was sentenced in Kiev to five years imprisonment followed by five years exile, his crime: "damaging the interests of citizens under the pretext of religious activity". On May 9, 1976, rallies were organised in several countries to arouse and express public sympathy for Georgi Vins in particular and for Christians imprisoned in Communist countries. For instance about 7,000 gathered in Hyde Park, London. A petition signed by a quarter of a million people was taken from the gathering to the Russian Embassy by a member of Parliament, but the Soviet officials lacked the grace even to receive it.

Prokofiev, Kryuchkov and the E.C.B.

Together with Gennadi K. Kryuchkov and Georgi Vins, Prokofiev has been a leader of the Reform or unregistered Baptists who strongly oppose the State control of the A.U.C.E.C.B. Prokofiev is regarded as the pioneer of the Action Group which represents the leadership of the unregistered Baptists and which campaigns with great courage for their rights.

The group crystallised in 1960 and those belonging to it were nicknamed "Prokofievites". It is known now as the *Initsiativniki* (the *Initiative* group) and also the E.C.B. (Evangelical Christians and Baptists). When we say Baptists in Russia it is right to remember that in fact this is an amalgam of Brethren, Pentecostals, Mennonites, Baptists and others.

Kryuchkov has served a three-year prison sentence and soldiers on. Prokofiev has been subjected to a total of twenty years either in prison or in Siberia. He has suffered much persecution from the press.

Suffering for the Gospel includes forcible internment in mental hospitals for some, the confiscation of homes and prayer-houses for others. Children are humiliated and sometimes forcibly taken from their parents. In some instances prisoners are denied Bibles and the right to correspond with friends and relatives. The police are known for brutality and the churches of the A.U.C.E.C.B. are not exempt from vicious attacks.

The creaking machinery of brutal repression grinds on but it cannot destroy the faith of these Christians who are used by the Holy Spirit to win converts in public and in prison.[5]

What of the future?

In summing up the conflict with Communism we must recognise that we are not fighting against flesh and blood. There is a Satanic force to be reckoned with and not just a political system or an economic way of life. The battle is a spiritual one and it manifests itself in the way described in these pages. Right across Russia, a distance from east to west of six or seven thousand miles, there are believers who pray every Friday in particular for revival. These Christians look to their brethren in the West to support them and to intercede for them.

Will conditions always prevail as they do in Russia today? In 1968 we saw walls crumbling in Czechoslovakia. These walls were soon re-erected but the events in Czechoslovakia did show that there is a limit to the life of a repressive system. In Russia the State power is backed and supported by a clear-cut atheistic, political philosophy. Christians are persecuted because the Communists feel that their teachings erode faith in Communism. We who have freedom ought therefore to pray fervently that the eyes of many Communists will be opened to see the futility of their system, as well as the saving power of Jesus Christ who is able to save to the uttermost all who come to God by him.

REFERENCES

[1] There are of course other groups. One of the most interesting of these is the "Old Believers" who have paid for their fidelity with martyrdom and exile. Since 1650 they have stood apart from the main Orthodox denomination in Russia. Three million Old Believers survive in the Soviet Union today. An article in the *National Geographic* magazine (Sept. 1972) documents the settlement of some Old Believers in Alaska.

[2] *The Times*, front page article 25.8.72.

[3] *Baptist Times*, 10.8.72.

[4] *Religious Minorities in the Soviet Union*, 1960-70 Minorities Rights Group.

[5] *A Criminal becomes Christian in a Russian Prison*, by V. I. Kozlov, E.C.M., 11 pp., 5p. Describes how a hardened criminal was converted through one of the Baptist leaders (Nikolai Khraphov) while in prison.

SUGGESTED READING

Faith on Trial in Russia. Michael Bordeaux. Hodder. 192 pp. 40p. This is probably the best introduction to the subject of Baptists in Russia.

Christian Appeals from Russia. Rosemary Harris, Xenia Howard-Johnson. Hodder. 160 pp. 30p. Documented with photos is the martyrdom of N. K. Khmarah who was tortured to death in prison in 1964. His tongue had been cut out and his body bore the marks of sadism.

Religious Ferment in Russia. Michael Bordeaux. Macmillan. 255 pp. £3. This book documents such issues as the Krushchev Campaign, The Reformers Challenge to the State and the Constitution of the A.U.C.E.C.B.

Russian Christians on Trial. E.C.M. 48 pp. 15p. Our Lord said that in the hour of trial it will be given us what to say. This book recording the trial of believers in Soviet courts certainly proves this to be true.

Christianity in a Revolutionary Age. Vol. 4. 483 ff. K. S. Latourette. 568 pp. £1·50.

Georgi Vins, Three Generations of Suffering, An Autobiography. Hodder. 222 pp. 85p.

Discretion and Valour. Trevor Beeson. Fontana. 348 pp. 60p.

The Opium of the People. Michael Bordeaux. Faber. 244 pp. £1·50. Provides a balanced, comprehensive, overall survey of religion in the U.S.S.R. Highly recommended.

A History of the Baptists. R. G. Torbet. p. 181 ff. Between 1914 and 1923 the Baptists increased, asserts Torbet, from well over 100,000 to one million.

In 1792 William Carey published "An Enquiry into the obligation of Christians to use means for the conversion of the heathen". This treatise examined the Great Commission, outlined a history of missionary work and provided a world survey. Carey stressed the practical use of means. Forty-two years later, in 1834, at the age of seventy-three, Carey died, having wrought a great work. This included the colossal achievement of translating the whole Bible into Bengali, Oriya, Hindi, Marathi, Sanskrit and Assamese and important portions of the Scriptures in twenty-eight other languages.

Daniel's day was a dark day of gloomy captivity, yet Daniel's God was alive, unchangeable, and acting as the all and only wise God. He sent a dream of truth to the pagan king Nebuchadnezzar and the same dream with the interpretation to Daniel. In the dream the victory belongs to the stone, which stone is Christ and the people joined to him by faith. That stone has smitten the kingdoms of this world and is now growing into a great mountain which will fill the whole earth (Dan. 2: 34, 35).

In spite of the assurance of ultimate victory there are those who can see only darkness.

Now is a dark time. Now the apostles of gloom and despair have their day. Now they prophesy the soon-coming universal triumph of Apollyon. Now, it is true, we labour much but reap little. Now there is little fruit in the vine or wheat in the field. Now we toil all night and in the morning say, "Lord we have caught nothing!" But it was not always so. And even now in days of drought whence come all these worldwide? But the rains and harvests will come once more. The promises are ripe. They await fulfilment. Yes, in these last days it shall come to pass, that the mountain of the Lord's house shall be established in the top of the mountains, and shall be exalted in the hills; and all nations shall flow unto it (Is. 2: 2, Mic. 4: 1). Now we see the tiniest trickle. Then shall come the river flow irresistible. Hallelujah!

BAPTISTS
WORLDWIDE

THROUGH the quarterly magazine *Reformation Today*, published by Cuckfield Baptist Church in Sussex, contact has been made with Baptists in many parts of the world.   This bi-monthly journal concentrates on the outworking of reformation in doctrine, the believer's experience and the practice of the local church.   There is evidence of renewed faith throughout the English-speaking world in the truths which are outlined in the chapter "What Baptists believe".   This awakening in doctrine appears to be affecting other language groups.

Accurate statistics concerning Baptists in over 120 countries are not possible.   The *Baptist World Alliance* publishes figures, but in most instances these include only those affiliated to the Alliance.   Nevertheless, these statistics are useful in that they give an idea of where the Baptists as a whole are located.   The Brethren—known as Open Brethren or Christian Brethren—resemble Baptists in several respects.   They are numerous but are not included in the following figures, which are mostly drawn from those published in 1975 by the *Baptist World Alliance*.   It is stressed that these figures are very general.   They can be challenged, and doubtless surveys would result in more accurate results.   It is felt nevertheless that general statistics are better than none at all.

In some cases the statistics might represent nominal Baptists only, that is people who have little if any religious conviction but when asked what religion they profess will say Baptist.   This is especially so in areas where there is little cost to discipleship.   Even though Baptists in some areas may be nominal only as is the case with other denominations such as Anglican, Methodist or Presbyterian it does help to know where they are located.   Furthermore in some countries where they form a small minority such as in Eastern European or Muslim countries we can be fairly sure that they are very much alive and far from nominal.

It is also to be observed that churches in which biblical doctrine is stressed maintain a more consistent discipline than most other churches.   Statistics

C. H. Spurgeon

in such instances are more meaningful than in the case of churches which may boast of a membership of 200 or 300 when only half or less of the registered number are actually involved as active members. On the other hand in some areas, such as the southern states of America, membership may be almost as nominal as it is in State churches of other countries. The great majority may have recorded a decision for Christ but show no evidence of a saving change. Only if such factors are borne in mind are the statistics of any value.

World Baptist Population—Quarter Million Increase Reported

Baptists of the world increased in number during 1974 by 256,415, placing the total number of church members at 33,749,228, the *Baptist World Alliance* reported.

B.W.A. General Secretary Robert S. Denny noted that this is an increase of 2.7 million since the Baptist World Congress in 1970 at Tokyo. That congress launched a World Mission of Reconciliation Through Jesus Christ which was largely evangelistic.

The statistics were compiled by Carl W. Tiller, an associate secretary of the B.W.A. Tiller said the 33.7 million total is for baptised believers only. These are church members. He estimated the total Baptist community, including children of Baptist families and others with Baptist preference, at about 74 million.

This year's statistics counted churches for the first time. There are 138,281 such organised congregations, plus an additional estimated 15,000 preaching places or missions.

Among the eight regional areas in the Baptist compilation, seven showed increases for the year. The exception was Central America and the Caribbean Islands, where a drop of 1.6 per cent was attributed to technical corrections of data for Trinidad and Tobago.

The largest Baptist population is in North America, where a total of 29,681,927 members was reported. North America has 101,088 Baptist churches—about 73 per cent of the world total.

Baptists are in 141 "countries" throughout the world. Technically, this is 112 sovereign nations and 29 offshore dependencies. This is believed to be the widest dispersion of any Christian group besides the Roman Catholic church. The world totals are:

	Churches 1975	Membership 1975
North America	101,088	29,681,927
Asia	10,404	1,205,543
Europe	11,157	1,168,847
Africa	7,530	787,692
South America	4,470	512,379
Central America and Caribbean	1,572	199,042
Oceania	2,022	198,856
Middle East	38	1,542
	138,281	33,749,228

Tiller's report also listed the "top ten" countries in Baptist membership totals, which remain in the same sequence as a year ago:

	Churches 1975	Membership 1975
United States	99,272	29,462,482
India	6,205	760,853
Soviet Union	5,025	539,000
Brazil	3,417	442,217
Burma	2,733	308,095
United Kingdom	3,065	253,546
Zaire	1,015	246,469
Canada	1,477	189,506
Romania	1,037	160,000
Nigeria	834	146,339

The B.W.A. count includes Baptist churches not affiliated with the Alliance, as well as its own constituency. The breakdown on this basis is:

	Churches 1975	Membership 1975
In Alliance member bodies	114,711	29,079,581
Outside the Alliance	23,570	5,669,647
	138,281	34,749,228

Africa

A vigorous Reformed movement exists among Baptists in South Africa. By their sincerity and ability young ministers of European stock show promise of leadership which is desperately needed both now and in the future. The African peoples often show zeal for Christ, massacres, such as in the Congo, and Burundi, having produced some heroic martyrs. But there is widespread lack of sound, systematic teaching. Africans desperately need expository books but in most cases can ill-afford them: in any case, very few titles are available in vernacular languages. South Africa has an annual Evangelical and Reformed Conference, which is interdenominational, and multi-racial as well as monthly Reformed studies groups in Johannesburg, Durban and Capetown. The main leadership in this movement comes from Baptist pastors, several of whom have experienced the blessing of God upon their ministries.

The government of Zaire recently decreed that all the churches should be united. Those refusing this unity will not be recognised by the civil authorities. The present position therefore is ominous, as it is in Uganda where missionaries have been well advised to leave the country.

Algeria	3	210	
Angola	35	9,518	
Botswana	2	48	
Burundi	5	3,561	
Cameroon	1,416	89,108	
Cape Verdi Islands	4	200	
Central African Republic	600	40,000	
Chad	50	3,000	
Congo	100	6,000	
Dahomey	14	450	
Egypt	8	427	
Ethiopia	12	821	
Ghana	66	2,587	
Ivory Coast	46	3,565	
Kenya	431	22,815	
Lesotho	20	701	
Liberia	224	32,694	
Libya	1	325	
Malagasy Republic	10	292	
Malawi	828	55,218	

Mali	1	25
Morocco	—	—
Mozambique	42	2,967
Namibia (Southwest Africa)	3	191
Niger	8	250
Nigeria	834	146,339
Rhodesia	144	19,868
Rwanda	122	18,431
Senegal	—	2
Sierra Leone	8	1,206
South Africa	896	53,444
St. Helena	2	80
Swaziland	4	197
Tanzania	300	15,092
Togo	12	1,011
Uganda	148	7,831
Upper Volta	1	162
Zaire	1,015	246,469
Zambia	101	6,161

America—North

Such is the preoccupation in the United States and Canada with "formula" evangelism—"receiving Christ as Saviour" by means of prayer formula following three or four simple steps to salvation—that anyone questioning these practices is likely to be dubbed a "hyper-Calvinist". Shallow doctrine and methods have led to widespread nominal evangelicalism. In some cases disillusionment with Decisionism has led some evangelicals to a willingness to search the Scriptures. Considerable progress has been made in a group of Reformed Baptist Churches in New Jersey and Pennsylvania, spearheading a renewal of free grace practice in the northeastern areas of the United States.

A Reformed Baptist movement has emerged in other parts such as the West Coast and in the state of Michigan, while in the Southern states an increasing number of churches is expressing the old truths in a robust and healthy way. The expression of this movement in Canada is modest but likewise showing increase.

America—South and Central

With the exception of Brazil, which is Portuguese speaking, the whole of South and Central America is Spanish speaking. Mexico, while geographically in the north, really belongs to the Spanish-speaking complex of the south.

The number of Protestants has increased in a dramatic fashion in Latin America. In 1900 it was 50,000; in the 1930s the number exceeded 1,000,000. In the 1940s it passed 2,000,000 and in the next decade leaped beyond the 5,000,000 mark. In the 1960s the increase continued so as to exceed 10,000,000. Now in the 1970s the number is well over 20,000,000. The number of Baptists is small compared with this total which contains a massive Pentecostal majority. Inasmuch as Pentecostals for the most part practise believers' baptism, are evangelical and have the same form of church order they are similar to Baptists. Yet the difference between Baptists and Pentecostals is basically a difference of authority and should on no account be under-estimated. This issue is discussed in the final chapter. Suffice it to assert here that Baptists are essentially Bible-based and not dream and vision centred. We do not live by direct revelations from heaven but by every word that is written in Scripture. Nowhere are these differences more clearly brought into focus than in South America where the need for expository preaching is paramount. The translation of the best commentaries on Scripture and the multiplication and distribution of Bible-centred books in lieu of sensational type books is a work designed to bring the highest good to the multitudes of Latin America.

There are a few who pray for and work toward an accomplishment of such a vision. For instance Bill Barkley, formerly of Manaus, has been working to establish an evangelical library and literature centre in Sao Paulo, Brazil.

South America

Argentina	..	396	24,732
Bolivia ..	..	156	8,400
Brazil ..	..	3,417	442,217
Chile ..	..	166	13,200
Colombia	..	85	7,561
Ecuador..	..	46	2,315
Guyana ..	..	27	2,093
Paraguay	..	25	2,376
Peru	..	47	3,381
Surinam..	..	4	213
Uruguay	..	52	2,501
Venezuela	..	49	3,390

Central America

El Salvador	..	42	3,252
Guatemala	..	83	5,836
Honduras	..	82	3,504
Nicaragua	..	60	5,108
Panama (and Canal Zone)	..	52	6,905
Trinidad and Tobago ..		24	2,263

Central America and Caribbean Islands

Antigua	..	2	120
Belize ..	..	7	300
Bahamas	..	278	25,688
Barbados	..	5	167
British Virgin Islands ..		2	120
Costa Rica	..	50	4,573
Cuba ..	..	192	14,924
Dominica	..	3	83
Dominican Republic ..		14	2,806
Grenada	..	—	—
Guadeloupe	..	4	72

Haiti ..	..	179	77,468
Jamaica	..	380	32,508
Martinique	..	9	500
Puerto Rico	..	73	11,450
St. Kitts/Nevis/Anguilla		4	240
St. Lucia	..	5	90
St. Vincent	..	4	80
Turks and Caicos Islands	..	10	785
U.S. Virgin Islands	..	8	200

Mr. Geoffrey Williams (1887-1975), founder of the Evangelical Library in London with branches all over the world, was converted through the preaching of J. K. Popham (see diagram pp. 40 and 41). Mr. Williams was a pure bibliophile—an avid reader, lover and collector of books. While he cherished his own heritage as a Baptist he sought out rare and valuable volumes on revivals wherever manifested in history saying that, "the greatest leaders of revival have always testified to the help and inspiration which they have received from the records of previous visitations of grace. The force of these facts has led me to spare no pains in collecting every work connected with those times of God's special favour." Mr. Williams regarded the Puritan writers with high esteem with the result that the Evangelical Library, 78a Chiltern Street in London's West End has one of the finest collections of Puritan volumes in the world.

Asia

In 1950 there were about one million Protestants in China. Little reliable information is now available about the true position in this nation of 800 million, the country with the largest population in the world. It has been judged that Baptists at one time numbered about 120,000. Newspapers in Hong Kong reported in September 1972 that the Communists were increasing pressures upon all religious bodies in an effort to destroy all religion in China. Such news sometimes comes from those who have managed to escape to Hong Kong.

India has about 760,000 Baptists. At a Reformed Conference in Britain in 1971, a Baptist missionary described how, since the time of William Carey's pioneering efforts, little indigenous work of a free grace nature has taken root. Nominal Christianity is a serious problem in India. As is universally the case, there is paramount need in India for excitement about God's great redemption in Christ and the sovereign grace of God which is exalted in salvation through Jesus Christ.

As in other parts of the world, there are signs in Asia among both missionaries and indigenous pastors of a return to the truths spelled out in the 1689 Baptist Confession of Faith.

Bangladesh	277	16,151	Macao	3	620
Burma	2,733	308,095	Malaysia	41	4,579
China, Republic of			Pakistan	24	2,253
(Taiwan)	84	13,115	Ryukyu Islands	32	2,884
Hong Kong	53	26,878	Singapore	11	1,624
India	6,205	760,853	Sri Lanka	21	2,010
Japan	334	33,020	Thailand	87	7,988
Korea, Republic of	476	23,615	Vietnam, Republic of	21	1,817
Laos	2	41			

Europe

Western Europe, once the scene of the stupendous impulse we call the Reformation, now has little evangelical strength. Decimated first by the unbelief of Modernism and then by the disguised unbelief and universalism of neo-orthodoxy or Barthianism, what was once a land of springs of water has now become parched ground, the habitation of dragons and unconverted clergy.

In this wilderness the Baptists, theologically speaking, are a feeble folk. They seem to have lost sight of the fact that the victory in the first place was a theological victory over Rome. What is required now is a theological victory over the various forms of liberal theology that have captured churches, colleges, universities and seminaries. Even Rome has been torn apart by Liberalism. Italy, one of her strong bastions, is now predominantly Communistic, rather than Romanist.

Ours is a warfare in the realm of truth. Without a sharp two-edged sword and the aptitude to use it, no victories can be anticipated. Yet one looks in vain for any centre or place of learning from where Baptist leaders are emerging. Perhaps the seminary way of forging leaders is being laid aside and God intends to raise up self-trained leaders from the churches.

The number of Baptists in Southern European countries is small, Spain 9,072, Portugal 3,386, Italy 5,449 and France 3,745 in 70 churches. From a Reformed point of view there are quite a few pastors of robust character in Spain but very few indeed in Italy and Portugal. Reformed Baptist churches are emerging in France including such centres as Marseilles, Montpellier and Paris.

Pastor Guy Appere leads a Reformed Baptist church in Geneva. He has contributed, as an author, to the increasing number of Reformed books being published in French which are distributed not only in France but in French-speaking areas of Africa.

Numerically, the Baptists are stronger in Scandinavian countries but it would seem that the Scandinavian temperament is doubly resistant to Calvinism, for such teaching is as rare there as giraffes or zebras. Latterly a Swedish Reformed Baptist magazine *Det Star Skrivet* has been making its mark.

In Britain a steady decline of standards and of membership continues in the Baptist Union. Churches continue to secede because of the hopeless apostasy of the Union, which apostasy was highlighted by the public denial of the divinity of Christ in 1971 by Michael Taylor, a tutor of the Northern Baptist College. The decline of the hyper-Calvinist stream (see diagram pp. 40 and 41) also continues unabated with churches closing down. Particular Baptists (the middle stream) show advance and, encouragingly, are uniting with the Reformed Baptist churches which are emerging in most parts of Britain.

The annual Carey Conference for ministers which began in 1970 with Herbert Carson as chairman continues to grow, being a source of strength and encouragement to the Reformed Baptists.

Austria ..	..	..	10	800	Netherlands ..	..	12	10,813
Belgium	..	..	12	538	Norway	..	..	65	6,659
Bulgaria..	..	..	20	1,000	Poland ..	..	..	52	2,401
Czechoslovakia	..	27	4,045	Portugal	..	..	56	3,386
Denmark	..	..	41	6,554	Romania	..	..	1,037	160,000
Finland ..	..	..	38	2,724	Spain ..	..	..	89	9,072
France ..	..	..	70	3,745	Sweden	..	..	708	44,687
Germany, Dem. Rep. of	222	22,535	Switzerland	..	..	24	2,822
Germany, Fed. Rep. of	371	69,433	U.S.S.R.	..	..	5,030	540,000
Greece ..	..	..	2	211	United Kingdom	..	2,977	252,315
Hungary	..	..	204	12,000	Yugoslavia	..	..	63	3,535
Iceland ..	..	..	1	50	Dependencies:			
Ireland, Republic of ..	8	250	Channel Islands	..	6	300
Italy	..	..	102	5,449	Isle of Man ..	..	1	27
Luxembourg	..	..	1	20				

97

South-West Pacific

As in South Africa, the Baptist world of Australia, in contrast to the Baptist Union in England, is evangelical and alert concerning the dangers of the modern Ecumenical movement. Increasing numbers of ministers have come to appreciate the benefits of the Reformation with its great wealth of expository literature. Men of firm faith and all-round ability are active. To a lesser extent the same is true of New Zealand.

Australia	..	..	699	50,306	Micronesia	..	3	185
Fiji	..	..	—	—	New Zealand ..	..	164	18,049
Guam ..	..	..	23	1,860	Papua New Guinea	..	221	11,930
Indonesia	..	..	122	30,011	Philippines	..	790	86,515

Communist-dominated Europe

To describe conditions in Communist countries is no easy matter since the situation varies from year to year and from area to area within any one country. If one speaks of freedom it is not unlikely that an indignant letter will be received documenting cruel persecution. On the other hand harrowing instances of trials may be cited in regard to some of these nations and this can result in accusations of exaggeration. Obviously the situation is complex, yet it is better to speak of these countries in a general way than run the risk of overlooking them, especially since the Christians in these countries should always be remembered in our prayers.

Albania, a small country of two million people, situated between Greece and Yugoslavia, is now called "Europe's most closed country". This is the area (Macedonia) where Paul's gospel once spread far and wide. Christianity was supposed to have been finally obliterated in Albania in 1967 when all the churches were closed. Today radio ministry is one way in which surviving believers may be receiving spiritual nourishment.

Poland in contrast to Albania has some freedom and that to the extent of an independent evangelical radio station. This is ironical in a way since this is more than Britain has! Preachers from the West have been able to preach at very well attended gatherings in Poland.

In Hungary faithful ministers of well established Reformed churches have been banished to isolated villages, their influence thus being terminated by the authorities. There appears to be an appetite for Bibles and Christian literature in Hungary and to some extent this demand is being met.

Since the invasion of Czechoslovakia by Russia in August 1968 the churches in that country have been subjected to a detailed government plan designed to limit their activities as much as possible. Propaganda against the churches has been intensified. Nevertheless visitors to Czechoslovakia report full and enthusiastic congregations in both cities and rural areas with a high proportion of young people attending. Numerically, Baptists are weak in the country but the number attending the churches is estimated at twice the number of church members which total is 4,045.

Conversions and progress are reported from Romania. Richard Wurmbrand in his books has shown how shocking conditions can be in that and other totalitarian states. Any encouragement that is reported must be received in the light that the freedom thermometer is seldom stationary. Renewed interest among Baptist pastors in the doctrines of grace is reported from Yugoslavia. Providing religious expression avoids political expression a measure of freedom is allowed to believers.

Darkness and tyranny prevail in Bulgaria. For evangelicals the position is very bleak.

Constant anti-Christian conditions and propaganda conspire to weaken testimony to the Gospel in East Germany.

It would be quite unrealistic not to face up to the enormous factors that militate against God's people in these countries. It is both vain and foolish to imagine that without the means of grace the churches will prosper. God *is* faithful. But that does not change the fact that his blessing of men consists firstly in providing the Scriptures and able preaching, and secondly, in making these means effective. If the first is absent the second is virtually impossible. It is a curse and a tragedy for any nation to lose its freedom. Let us cherish ours for we may not always have it.

That thou mayest know how thou oughtest to behave thyself in the house of God, which is the church of the living God, the pillar and ground of the truth (1 Timothy 3: 15). The only truth by which eternal salvation comes to men is to be held aloft as on a mighty column for all to see. The base from which this is to spring is the local church. The whole truth, clearly expressed as instruction for all living is to be cherished and the church regarded as the guardian of it. All God's counsel is to be preserved and handed on to our children's children through the local church. A higher responsibility entrusted to the pastors could hardly be conceived. How wretched therefore it is to trifle with any part of God's Word or disclaim the place of doctrine.

WHAT
BAPTISTS BELIEVE

THE verdict of historical theology is that Baptists adhere tenaciously to the fundamentals of the Christian faith as held by the Protestant churches at large from the Reformation onwards. Here, however, we can do little more than point to six main beliefs distinctive of Baptist testimony. David Kingdon has outlined them as follows:

1. The Supremacy of Scripture
2. Regenerate Church Membership
3. The Voluntary Nature of Discipleship
4. The Baptism of Believers by Immersion
5. The Headship of Christ
6. The Priesthood and Prophethood of all Believers.

In developing these themes Mr. Kingdon points out that the doctrinal heritage has resulted in certain characteristics in the practical realm; for instance, a strong emphasis has been laid on the separation of Church and State. This stems from the view of Christ as Head of the Church. He rules his Church through elders and not through secular politicians. Hence the Baptists have been able, to a remarkable degree, to survive political changes in their respective geographical locations. They have been characterised by a strong emphasis on evangelism which is largely the outworking of the belief that all believers are responsible to witness to, and to pray for, the unconverted.

During the latter half of the 19th Century a decline set in among Baptists in general—there are notable exceptions—and this has continued to the present day. A similar decline, in some cases tragic in the extreme, is to be seen in all the major denominations and is due mainly to the advance of Liberalism, formerly called Modernism. The first-named distinctive doctrinal feature noted above, that is, the supremacy of Scripture, has been widely queried, and by many virtually abandoned. The belief in the plenary inspiration and divine authority of "the Word written" has largely been forsaken and dubbed "obscurantism". Such is the influence of the

101

thinking which is critical of biblical authority that today even the Roman Catholic Church is divided in a radical way over this very issue, liberals taking one side and conservatives the other.

A further major issue concerns the way of salvation. Baptists believe in a regenerate Church membership. But what exactly is regeneration?— and how are men and women saved? On these questions a drastic difference has emerged in that the majority of present-day Baptists reject, consciously or unconsciously, the axiom of the Reformed Faith, that regeneration is altogether an act of God. They maintain that God is unable to regenerate a man until the man is willing, or until he decides for Christ. At this point the clash between Arminianism and Calvinism comes into view. It must, of course, be resolved biblically, but there is wisdom in looking at it in its historic setting, and attention is given to the matter in the following pages.

It is to the credit of the Baptists that, in their history, they have followed the Reformers' main teachings, which are to be found enunciated clearly in the Baptist Confession drawn up in London in 1677 and published in 1689. To understand the Baptists it is vital to understand Reformation principles, for 17th Century Baptists in general believed all the doctrines taught by the Reformers and Puritans, even though they failed to agree with them on the subject of baptism. What actually happened at the time of the Reformation is explained in the First Chapter of this book. The present revival of interest in the theology of the Reformers among Baptists of the English-speaking world renders the subject doubly important.

For between one hundred and fifty and two hundred years the 1689 Confession remained the definitive confession of faith of the Particular Baptist churches in England and Wales. The chart illustrating English Baptist history shows the Particular Baptist stream, which is experiencing considerable renewal today in different parts of the world. Churches today are adopting the 1689 Confession as their doctrinal standard, sometimes with minor amendments.[1]

In contrast, many Baptists are indifferent to creeds since they see no need for them, while others are hostile to their use. Such open themselves to the charge that they do not know what they believe or that they are unable to articulate what they believe, or worse still the truth means so little to them that they do not care to state and defend it. By and large their assertions carry weight, for it is rare to find an able and bold defender of the faith who at the same time rejects the place of confessions of faith.

C. H. Spurgeon would have had little time for the spineless and uninspiring leadership so much in evidence today. He felt strongly about doctrine. At the commencement of his ministry in London he published the 1689 Confession, heartily commending it to his flock. "This little volume," he wrote in the foreword, "is not issued as an authoritative rule, or code of faith, whereby you are to be fettered, but as an assistance to you in controversy, a confirmation in faith, and a means of edification in righteousness. Here the younger members of our church will have a body of divinity in small compass, and by means of the scriptural proofs, will be ready to give a reason for the hope that is in them.

"Be not ashamed of your faith; remember it is the ancient gospel of martyrs, confessors, reformers and saints. Above all, it is *the truth of God*, against which the gates of Hell cannot prevail.

"Let your lives adorn your faith, let your example adorn your creed. Above all live in Christ Jesus, and walk in him, giving credence to no teaching but that which is manifestly approved of him, and owned by the Holy Spirit. Cleave fast to the Word of God which is here mapped out for you."

As we consider the subject of what Baptists believe, ten important points will now be drawn out of the 1689 Confession as being of particular relevance. Other truths such as justification, the nature of saving faith, adoption, sanctification, good works, perseverance and assurance are not overlooked. In defending a country the borders most subject to attack are strengthened. Care is needed to strengthen those areas of truth where the enemy is concentrating his attack. We do well to remember that truth is a unity. If a break is made in the walls the whole city is subject to collapse. Likewise with Scripture. Give up one truth and it will not be long before everything is lost.

1. The Holy Scriptures

It is one thing to assert that the Scriptures are supreme; it is another to spell out what this means in precise terms. The 1689 Confession declares that the Hebrew Scriptures of the Old Testament, and the Greek of the New, were immediately inspired by God. Even this is inadequate. Scripture is God-breathed. The Scriptures come directly from God and therefore in their original form are perfect and infallible.

Prof. William Barclay in the *Baptist Times*[2] rejects this view. He uses the popular method of Modernists which is to ridicule the idea that God literally dictated Scripture to the original penman. Of course we do not believe in a dictation theory and regard the compromised position put forward by Prof. Barclay as totally unsatisfactory since it is the position upon which all criticisms of the Bible are based, *i.e.* the Bible contains mistakes and contradictions and reliance upon it, therefore, is limited.

In describing the history of Scripture subsequent to its writing, the wording of the Confession is apt; it was "by (God's) singular care and providence kept pure in all ages", and is "to be translated into the vulgar language of every nation . . ." Ch. 1 Sect. 8.

2. God's decree

What could be more important in an age of confusion and uncertainty than the knowledge that God is exercising his all-wise purpose and control in all events? This the Confession states as follows:

"God hath decreed in himself, from all eternity, by the most wise and holy counsel of his own will, freely and unchangeably, all things, whatsoever comes to pass; yet so as thereby is God neither the author of sin nor hath any fellowship with any therein; nor is violence offered to the will of the creature, nor yet is the liberty or contingency of second causes taken away." Ch. 3 Sect. 1.

Belief in the sovereignty of God is to the Christian faith what bones are to the human body. A strong athlete must have a robust frame. If we believe that God is weak or feeble or not in control, this will undermine faith. Gresham Machen, one of the foremost evangelical leaders of this century declared:

"The more I have looked out upon the state of the Church at the present time, the more I have contemplated recent church history, the more firmly I am convinced that error regarding predestination leads inevitably to more and more error, and often constitutes the entering wedge by which the entire Christian testimony of individuals and of churches is undermined."[3]

One widespread idea is that God foresaw what would happen in the world and then decreed that this is what should happen! This untenable notion is specifically countered in the next clause, "yet hath he not decreed anything because he foresaw it as future". Scripture texts are supplied throughout and in this instance Romans 11: 11, 13, 16, 18 is included.

3. Creation

Enormous pressures are brought to bear upon Bible-believing people because of the popular pseudo-scientific philosophy of evolution. Our age is secularly-minded, materialistic and anti-supernaturalistic. It is therefore of first importance that believers work within a framework of thought in which the structure of faith is supported by the solid and immovable columns of supernaturalism. The very essence of true belief is faith in the absolute Godhood of God.

God made all things out of nothing. This is supernatural. The hour draws near when the universe will be rolled up like a scroll, when there will be a universal resurrection of the righteous and unrighteous and the creation of a new heavens and new earth. This also is supernatural.

"In the beginning it pleased God . . . to create or make the world, and all things therein, whether visible or invisible, in the space of six days," declares the Confession. But what if some scientists claim that the Bible is wrong since it has been disproved by the findings of science? The answer is that science is inadequate, particularly in this sphere where we are confronted with the supernatural! Scientific findings are always subject to change as more knowledge is discovered. The Bible, in contrast, has stood the test of centuries and will triumph in this age also.

4. The Fall of Man

Influenced by the theory of evolution, some regard the creation account as merely symbolic and Adam and Eve as merely symbolic figures. Others regard Adam and Eve as the first apes to become human in the evolutionary chain. The Confession speaks clearly of Adam and Eve as two people made by an act of creation; two people who fell into sin; two people from whom all men have descended. By the first transgression all mankind became "dead in sin, and wholly defiled in all the faculties and parts of soul and body". Ch. 6 Sect. 1.

5. The Divinity of Christ

In April 1971, Rev. Michael Taylor used the annual assembly platform of the Baptist Union in England to make the following statement: "I am not troubled or surprised that he (Jesus) doesn't know everything or sometimes makes a mistake, or gets angry, or doesn't have all the gifts, or betrays himself as a child of his time. However remarkable his life, I think I must stop short of saying categorically: Jesus is God. So first, Jesus is a man like you and me, and second God is present and active in Jesus as he is present and active in us all."

When such heresy is rampant and no action taken to discipline the heretic the relevance of the Confession can be appreciated. It declares: "The Son of God, the second person in the Holy Trinity, being very and eternal God, the brightness of the Father's glory, of one substance and equal with him who made the world, who upholdeth and governeth all things he hath made, did, when the fulness of time was come, take upon him man's nature, with all the essential properties and common infirmities thereof, yet without sin." Ch. 8 Sect. 2.

6. Free-will

Of paramount need is an understanding of the biblical doctrine of man. Free-will is the arch error of modern evangelicalism. Decisionism— declaring people believers on the grounds of a decision made—is rife. When we speak about free-will we mean the notion that all men are free to decide for Christ at any time and that becoming a Christian is very easy and simple. In public meetings this can lead often to the manipulation of people in order to make them come forward to register a decision. This decision is supposed to save them because it opens the door for God, who cannot, according to "free-willism", work the new birth until the sinner himself takes the initiative. The 1689 Confession counters this error:

"Man, by his fall into a state of sin, hath wholly lost all ability of will to any spiritual good accompanying salvation; so as a natural man, being altogether averse from that good, and dead in sin, is not able by his own strength to convert himself, or to prepare himself thereunto." Ch. 9 Sect. 3.

7. Effectual Calling

In the light of the above it can be seen that an understanding of the new birth is important. In calling sinners from their state of spiritual deadness, God regenerates them. Note the power and clarity of the following statement in the Confession. The biblical references are included since these Scriptures, when examined, clinch this issue beyond refutation:

"Those whom God hath predestinated unto life, he is pleased in his appointed and accepted time, effectually to call,[4] by his Word and Spirit, out of that state of sin and death in which they are by nature, to grace and salvation by Jesus Christ;[5] enlightening their minds spiritually and savingly to understand the things of God;[6] taking away their heart of stone, and giving unto them a heart of flesh:[7] renewing their wills, and by his almighty power determining them to that which is good, and effectually drawing them to Jesus Christ;[8] yet so as they come most freely, being made willing by his grace."[9] Ch. 10 Sect. 1.

8. Repentance to life and salvation

The following conversation typifies much evangelism of the present era:
"The Bible declares that all men are sinners. Do you believe that?"
"Yes."
"Then *you* must be a sinner?"
"Yes."
"The Bible says that Christ died to save sinners and that if we call on Christ to save us he will. Do you believe that?"
"Sure."
"Then are you ready to call on God after me in prayer?"
"I suppose so."
A prayer follows.
"Praise the Lord, brother, now you are saved. You are, aren't you?"
"I suppose so."
"What do you mean, 'I suppose so'? God cannot lie. He says if we call on him he will save us. You have called on him and you are saved. Now you must read the Bible every day, you must pray daily, you must tell people that Christ has saved you. The Bible says that if we believe and if we confess Christ with our mouths we will be saved."

This is the popular method of soul-winning. It has been simplified but then oversimplification of the Gospel is the order of the day. Bad preaching is recognised not so much by what is said as by what is omitted.

The omission of repentance in preaching or in soul-winning is bad. It is not only bad, it is fatal. Noah, the prophets, John the Baptist, Christ,

106

the apostles and the great preachers of this dispensation have been faithful in preaching the necessity of repentance. Neglect of this truth ruins thousands. Omission of repentance fills churches with tares instead of wheat.

Without true repentance or a change of heart, there can be no salvation. Because repentance involves a change of heart it is no easy matter. The Confession says of repentance: "This saving repentance is an evangelical grace, whereby a person, being by the Holy Spirit made sensible of the manifold evils of his sin, doth, by faith in Christ, humble himself for it with godly sorrow, detestation of it, and self-abhorrence. . . ." Ch. 15 Sect. 3.

Repentance is comprehensive. It effects a change in every part of man's nature. It involves a turning from all human sins and not just some sins. Repentance is not just sorrow for sin. It includes that, but essentially repentance is turning to God. It is something which continues throughout life.

When the Confession declares that repentance is "an evangelical grace" it means that it is implanted by God and worked in man because of grace. Repentance is a gift. Acts 11: 18; Zech. 12: 10.

9. The law of God

Together with repentance, preaching of the moral law or ten commandments has fallen into neglect. The two go together. By the law is a knowledge of sin. Rom. 3: 20. The second and seventh chapters of Romans are key chapters of Scripture explaining the place and necessity of the law.

Many complain that there is little sense or conviction of sin today even among professing Christians. How can there be, unless the moral law of God is proclaimed and pressed home upon the consciences of men and women?

The moral law is not only imperative in Gospel preaching but is essential for the establishment of believers in the faith. The Confession states this well when it says:

"The moral law doth for ever bind all, as well justified persons as others, to the obedience thereof, and that not only in regard of the matter contained in it, but also in respect of the authority of God the Creator, who gave it; neither doth Christ in the Gospel any way dissolve, but much strengthen this obligation." Ch. 19 Sect. 5.

10. The last judgment and everlasting punishment

The truth of everlasting punishment of the wicked which is taught clearly and repeatedly by our Lord and by the apostles is regarded with hostility by those who think naturally rather than spiritually. For this reason preachers are tempted to tone down the doctrine and assert that the wicked are annihilated or destroyed. This was the chief issue raised by Spurgeon in the Downgrade controversy and is very much a live issue today. When efforts were made in January 1972 to form a new Association of Evangelical Baptist Churches in London, because of the upheaval in the Baptist Union, it was the denial of eternal punishment (admittedly by a minority present) which hindered progress.

Many reasons can be given to support the major importance of the truth of the great coming day of judgment, to be followed by the eternal retribution of the wicked. This truth shows the enormity of sin. It points to the inscrutable justice of God. It emphasises the reality of the cross of Christ. If God was willing that his Son should suffer and die for sin, it certainly indicates that he will in no wise acquit the wicked. The doctrine shows that there is no hope of human nature becoming regenerate after death. If a man dies with a God-hating nature he will have a God-hating nature for all eternity, and will, in the words of the Confession, "be cast aside into everlasting torments". Ch. 32 Sect. 2.

Finally this truth underlines the urgency of evangelism. The means of grace must be employed to the fullest extent possible, for it is by preaching that God saves sinners from every kindred, tongue, people and nation.

REFERENCES

[1] It is surprising how little in a confession of some fifty-four pages needs alteration. The section on Scripture requires additional clarification because of present-day neo-orthodoxy. Chapter 10 Section 3 concerning the regeneration of infants does not accord with the convictions of some, while others are unhappy about the equating of the pope with anti-Christ—Chap. 26 Sect. 4.
[2] August 31, 1972.
[3] *The Christian View of Man*, p. 59.
[4] Rom 8: 30; 11: 7; Eph. 1: 10, 11; 2 Thess. 2: 13, 14.
[5] Eph. 2: 1-6.
[6] Acts 26: 18; Eph. 1: 17, 18.
[7] Ezek. 36: 26.
[8] Deut. 30: 6; Ezek. 36: 27; Eph. 1: 19.
[9] Ps. 110: 3; Song 1: 4.

BAPTISTS AND
THE WAY AHEAD

EPHESUS was the third main base for the spread of the Gospel during the apostolic era. After the beginning of the church in Jerusalem, Antioch in Syria became the second springboard of missionary outreach to the Gentile world. From Antioch Paul and his companions went forward. To Antioch they returned. When Paul set out from Antioch for the third time, an important event in the history of the church was to take place. This was the establishment at Ephesus of a centre from which the whole of Asia Minor was evangelised. Ephesus was the largest and most important city in that whole region, acting as the gateway to the hinterland. Some of the churches established from Ephesus are mentioned in the book of Revelation, namely, Smyrna, Pergamos, Thyatira, Sardis, Philadelphia and Laodicea. The whole of Paul's tremendous ministry at Ephesus is summed up in a sentence, "so mightily grew the word of God and prevailed" (Acts 19: 20).

The "word of God" grew, grew mightily, and prevailed. If this were to happen in all nations today as it did in Asia Minor, then we would be in what is popularly called the millennium, a period—not necessarily a thousand years—which some expect before the end of the world.

What is the "word of God"? This can be understood as the whole teaching of Scripture. It can also refer to the person of the Lord Jesus who is the spirit, life and soul of the word of God written (John 1: 1-14). To interpret the "word of God" as the "commands of God" would not be wrong but is not comprehensive enough in meaning. A fuller definition of the "word of God" as it is expressed in Acts 19: 20 is "the doctrinal, experimental and practical knowledge of union with God the Father, God the Son and God the Holy Spirit". This union is expressed in believers' baptism.

Paul gathered the converts into churches and set elders over each church, as we see in the next chapter which describes the calling of the elders of Ephesus to Miletus where Paul instructs them for the last time (Acts 20:

17-38). The custom of the apostles to establish a plurality of elders in each church is confirmed by this passage as it is by other parts of Scripture. Acts 14: 23 is an instance in which it is specifically declared that elders were ordained in every church. The apostles were extraordinary both in office and gifts and with their deputies, the evangelists who assisted them, had authority to appoint elders in this way. The manner in which elders are recognised is explained in the pastoral epistles (Titus 1; 1 Tim. 3).

A review of the work at Ephesus reveals four ways in which the word of God prevailed, and that mightily, these comprehending the work as a whole:

1. In preaching—illustrated by the school of Tyrannus (Acts 19: 9).
2. In evangelism—the whole of Asia Minor was evangelised (Acts 19: 10).
3. In church order—elderships were established (Acts 20: 17, 28).
4. In reformation of life—bad books were burned and idols abolished (Acts 19: 19, 26).

Baptists make it their boast that for them the Word of God is supreme. But examination of present day practice in the light of Scripture shows that much is far removed from the New Testament.

1. The Word of God should prevail mightily in preaching

The Word of God grows when it is translated into different languages, distributed and read. It prevails when its meaning and message is understood and obeyed. The most powerful vehicle by which the Word grows and prevails, however, is through preaching. "It pleased God through the foolishness of preaching to save them that believe." The authority and power of God is expressed in preaching when the truth of Scripture is proclaimed in the power of the Holy Spirit. God's mind and will is expressed in this way above all other ways. Through such preaching, power is imparted by which sinners both will and do God's good pleasure.

It is the testimony of those who have heard such preaching that nothing in this world can compare with it. It is a dynamic power by which people are transformed in the whole of their outlook and practice.

This kind of preaching is all too rare in Baptist circles today. In many instances a man will announce a text, and after a few observations concerning it, proceed to recount anecdotes or narrate entertaining stories. Needless to say, such trifling deserves the strongest censure. Yet these impostures have prevailed to the extent that perhaps a majority of evangelicals have become conditioned to this kind of fare. The result is that they have little appetite for preaching which demands concentration, convicts them, and calls them to wholehearted devotion and discipline.

A far more sinister way in which the Word of God has been made null and void is through the advance of Modernism. Modernism is the name used to describe the unbelief which masquerades under the name of theology and which is really a denial of the supernatural acts of God recorded in the Bible, such as the virgin birth, the resurrection of Christ, and the miracles. The Holy Spirit will honour only that which is true and faithful. Modernism has spread through men who have felt that the Scriptures make unreasonable demands upon them and that their explanations, in which large sections of the Bible are viewed as myths, offer a viable alternative to evangelical Christianity.

Modernism, which has been the greatest hindrance to the growth of the Word of God, spread rapidly among the Baptists during the last century. In C. H. Spurgeon, Modernism found a most powerful enemy. The battle came to a climax in the famous downgrade controversy. Now, eighty years later, the Southern Baptists of America are experiencing a similar crisis.

The Southern Baptist Convention represents the greatest numerical force of Baptists ever known (about twelve million). The controversy centres around the publication of a twelve-volume commentary on Scripture which is Modernistic. This is published by the Southern Baptist Convention's Sunday School Board.[1] Because of the commentary's espousal of "higher" criticism (e.g. the book of Esther may be fictional; Jesus did not walk on the water, etc.) the Convention passed a resolution in 1970 that the commentary should be withdrawn and rewritten.[2]

At the annual convention held in Philadelphia in 1972 the battle was re-fought and this time was won by the liberals. An editorial in *Christianity Today* commented that the Convention was not faced with questions of interpretation, or of Calvinism versus Arminianism and the like, but rather, "what is at stake here is the trustworthiness of the Bible—the action of the 1972 Convention compromises this controlling principle and opens the floodgates to all kinds of serious theological error—the pages of history abound with examples of what happens when the full fruit of such a viewpoint is harvested—theological liberal seminaries, defective churches, a declining interest in evangelism, and at last apostasy. This will be the unhappy course of the Southern Baptist Convention if the present action is not reversed in the future."[3]

Preaching the whole counsel of God includes the clearest expression of the way of salvation—repentance toward God and faith in the Lord Jesus Christ—but also includes all biblical doctrine, particularly where truth is being attacked or neglected. Areas of faith under attack are suggested in the chapter, "What Baptists Believe".

The Word of God prevails mightily when preachers are given the authority and unction of the Holy Spirit to stress much application as they expound the Scriptures. About half of Paul's address to the Ephesian elders refers to his own example in practice. With all humility of mind he could claim that his example was a living epitome of the truth he proclaimed. His epistle to the Ephesians is not lacking in application. "Let him that stole steal no more," and many other lessons follow as the logical outcome of doctrine.

In England, when ministers turn back to the old truths, there is a tendency for them to proclaim doctrines without adequate application. The power, relevance and significance of truth is felt most when applied to daily life. In this way the Word prevails mightily, and it is in this area that the Reformed Baptist movement of the future will either stand or fall.

2. The Word of God should prevail mightily in evangelism

When Paul said that he was pure of the blood of all men because he had not shunned to preach the whole counsel of God, he meant that nothing needful for the spiritual birth and spiritual growth of souls had been withheld. Everything by which salvation could be secured had been taught. The Word prevailed in his evangelism. Teaching was inextricably bound up with the message of salvation.

The popular method which pertains in evangelism in most Baptist churches today is that of calling for decisions. Salvation has been over-simplified so as to bypass repentance. Faith in Christ is still stressed, although even here little enough teaching is provided as to who Christ is. "Smile, Jesus loves you" is the idea that is often conveyed. Decide for Jesus, join his side, stand for him. Opportunity to register a decision is given at the end of meetings and appeals are made for people to come to the front and sign a card.

It is erroneously thought that a decision is essential before God can regenerate the soul. Thus a new kind of serious error, if not heresy, has overrun evangelism, just as Arianism overran Christendom in the time of Athanasius. Regeneration precedes repentance and faith (John 1: 12, 13). Visualise two men in a meeting. One is regenerate and shows genuine repentance and the good works of saving faith in his life (James 2: 18-26). The other is unregenerate. Having clear views about the new birth the pastor never makes altar-calls, but one day a visiting preacher makes such an appeal. Both characters feel constrained to respond and both register a decision. Subsequently the pastor observes that apart from some confused thinking absolutely nothing has happened. The one man is still born again and the other not.

There is an immense difference between true faith and easy believism or what can be called mere intellectual assent. Finney and those who have copied his methods have used the altar call to bring men to make what is often a merely human response, which does not spring from spiritual rebirth. It is significant that this means of inducing a response has no warrant from Scripture. The apostles did not do it. They commanded repentance. They entreated, they reasoned and they pleaded, but they never made an altar call. Why? The answer is that the Holy Spirit does his own invincible work in sinners. If we attempt to do this work for him, it will inevitably result in false converts who have responded to us but not to the truth. The altar call is an unscriptural device which evangelists have used to advertise their success. Many thousands, perhaps millions, of professions of conversion have been made which have come to nothing and resulted in deep disillusionment. Altar-call results, which advertise large numbers of conversions, constitute a great lie and a wicked scandal in modern Christian life.

These are strong statements. They are countered by the claim that even a few genuine conversions make the whole system worthwhile, to which we reply that the biblical method results in the same conversions without an aftermath of confusion and disillusionment. Nevertheless, neglect of the whole counsel of God has not only led to wrong methods of evangelism but is also responsible for shallow teaching in the churches. A preacher who insists on what we call the doctrines of grace faces ominous opposition since such proclamation contradicts popular belief and challenges popular practice.

Many who may have doubts about the altar call think of Billy Graham and come to the conclusion that the altar call method must be right since he has employed it with such success. Not only is this success to be questioned and challenged but there are other aspects of Crusade evangelism which create perplexity for evangelicals, particularly evangelical ministers.

The dilemma facing an evangelical Baptist pastor when confronted with a united evangelistic effort is three-fold. First, he cannot forsake the whole counsel of God to support methods such as the altar call and the use of sensational publicity which deny and undermine the truth. For this he will bear reproach and it is well for him if he provides an outstanding example of constant evangelism himself without relying on unscriptural aids. Second, he cannot forsake the whole counsel of God by joining with those of whom John writes, "If there come any unto you, and bring not this doctrine (the doctrine of Christ as God and Man), receive him not into your house, neither bid him God speed: for he that biddeth him God speed is partaker of his evil deeds" (2 John 10, 11). How can he give public approval to those who deny the infallibility of the original Scriptures? How can he bid God speed to those who deny the Godhood of Christ? How can he make public prayer for, and unite on the same platform with, those who overthrow the doctrine of justification by faith, of whom Paul wrote, "Let them be anathema" (Gal. 1: 8)? Third, having a concern for the doctrine of the local, gathered church, and believing that to baptise converts and gather them into disciplined churches is part of the fulfilment of Christ's commission, he is most unhappy about the tendency in large campaigns to direct converts back to any and every kind of "church" in the area.

These issues were outlined in a paperback entitled *The Pastor's Dilemma* published in 1966.[4] Some may argue that the Arminianism[5] of modern evangelism is not serious. It is an error, they may say, but since people are saved through Arminian preaching it cannot be classed as heresy. Heresy is something which undermines the faith in a vital point so as to overthrow salvation, whereas error concerns mere details or non-essentials. It is true that Arminianism as it is commonly known is not heresy. But altar call decisionism as it is sometimes practised is heresy, for it assures decision-makers that they are regenerate when the marks of regeneration are hardly in evidence. This is to overthrow the doctrine of salvation and is heresy. Likewise the practice of Campus Crusade is blatant heresy for it omits the essential doctrine of repentance and thus destroys the doctrine of salvation.[6]

The Word of God should prevail in our evangelism. Spurgeon in an address on the subject of "Sermons likely to win souls" declares:

"A sermon must be instructive. If people are to be saved by a discourse, it must contain at least some measure of knowledge. There must be light as well as fire. Some preachers are all light, and no fire, and others are all fire and no light; what we want is both fire and light. I do not judge those brethren who are all fire and fury; but I wish they had a little more knowledge of what they talk about, and I think it would be well if they did not begin quite so soon to preach what they hardly understand themselves. It is a fine thing to stand up in the street, and cry, 'Believe! Believe! Believe! Believe! Believe! Believe!' Yes, my dear soul, but what have we to believe? What is all this noise about? Preachers of this sort are like a little boy who had been crying, and something happened that stopped him in the middle of his cry, and presently he said, 'Ma, please what was I crying about?' Emotion, doubtless, is a very proper thing in the pulpit, and the feeling, the pathos, the power of heart, are good and grand things in the right place; but do also use your brains a little, do tell us something when you stand up to preach the everlasting gospel.

"The sermons that are most likely to convert people seem to me to be those that are full of truth, truth about the fall, truth about the law, truth about human nature, and its alienation from God, truth about Jesus Christ, truth about the Holy Spirit, truth about the Everlasting Father, truth about the new birth, truth about obedience to God, and how we learn it, and all such great verities."[7]

The Word of God includes all the doctrines it contains. Nothing is to be kept back. All the truths outlined in the chapter, "What Baptists Believe", are included in the whole counsel of God.

Needless to say there must be outreach. We must have confrontation with unbelievers as Paul did in the market place daily at Athens (Acts 17:17). The social conditions of our time need intelligent study and our outreach should be planned so that every creature hears the Gospel message.[8] This is the work of the local church and such evangelistic outreach is best carried on when a church is spiritually strong and versatile. This leads us to our next consideration.

3. The Word of God must prevail in church order

The main question throughout the age has been, what is a Christian? Together with that question, the main issue of this century is, what is a church? The twentieth century has been noted for the great ecumenical movement,[9] a movement which is destined to futility for confusion reigns within it regarding both what is a Christian, and what is a church.

Baptists claim to be clear on both issues. A Christian is one who is born again of God's Spirit, who is united to Christ, and who shows the fruit of this union in his life. A church is an assembly of believers gathered together under the authority of Scripture. This concept is of course in opposition to the Anglican and Presbyterian practice in which vast numbers of nominal people are found in membership. A church, to be such, should have a proper oversight, faithful preaching and the practice of the ordinances of believers' baptism and the Lord's Supper.

History attests that if the leadership of a church is corrupt then decay will soon be seen in all departments. We cannot afford to under-estimate the importance of the eldership. In this alone Christ expresses his shepherding care. He is the chief shepherd. The elders are Christ's under-shepherds (1 Pet. 5: 1-5). To him they will give account (Heb. 13-17). No other permanent order for the care of the flock is revealed in the New Testament. If this breaks down the church breaks down, for no other provision is made for shepherding.

We have seen how the Scriptures grew mightily and prevailed in Ephesus and throughout Asia Minor. Paul's method was to plant churches, each having its own responsible leadership in the form of an eldership. In each church, thus constituted, lay a tremendous potential for planting further churches. For instance, to one of these churches, namely Philadelphia, our Lord said, "I have set before thee an open door, and no man can shut it." Philadelphia was situated on one of the main highways, a constant symbol beckoning them to reach out with the truth. A properly ordered church which is faithful in evangelism and which is careful to nurture converts, causing them to grow in grace, can be a mighty instrument in the Lord's hands. Doors of service are opened to them which no man can close.

That Paul called the elders of Ephesus to meet with him is most significant. He did not call the deacons to make the journey of about thirty miles to Miletus. He did not call heads of organisations. He did not call leaders of societies. He did not call lady missionaries. The only ones invited were those who were actually functioning in the churches as elders, whether overseeing elders (which all elders are), or teaching elders. It is likely that many, perhaps most of the elders called to Miletus, were full-time. To travel thirty or more miles and then return would have taken two or three days in all, and most people, irrespective of generation or country, are not able simply to down tools, leave their employment, and make an extended journey. Also it is likely that Paul followed our Lord's example recorded in Luke 10 when Jesus sent out seventy disciples, two by two, to evangelise all the villages and towns. For such a task a considerable force of elders would be necessary and we can imagine that the company of elders at Ephesus was considerable, perhaps thirty, forty, or more. Ephesus was not only the wealthiest, but the most cosmopolitan and heavily populated city in Asia. Some of our modern cities have ten or twenty evangelical churches. Why should we think there was only one in Ephesus? When Jesus addresses the angel of the church of Ephesus this angel can be taken as being a messenger.

Nor would it be out of place to regard the angel as representing the elders of the Ephesian churches in a symbolic sense. The use of the singular— *the church* at Ephesus—need not confuse the issue since it is not out of place to call a grouping of churches in a city, the church of that city. Evangelical unity is implicit in this idea but not central control, either by a synod or archbishop.

The important point to note is the fact that only one form of church government is described in Scripture—"elders in every church" (Acts 14: 23). Yet in so many cases today Baptist churches are ruled by deacons. Some large churches are ruled by one pastor or elder, the principle of plurality being conveniently ignored. We can understand small churches having one overseer only, but it is difficult to believe that one man alone can provide in an adequate way for the needs of a church when there may be a hundred or more members.

It is argued that so long as there is an order and discipline of some kind we can be thankful, and we need not worry about details. Some regard this question of church government as an open issue. They deny that the New Testament lays down specific order. Various traditional forms, therefore, have come to prevail. And within these traditional forms many unscriptural practices have come to prevail.

Entertainment has become prominent in worship services particularly in American churches. Song leaders are spoken of and have such an aura of indispensibility that anyone would think that Paul had commanded Timothy to ordain elders *and song-leaders* in all the churches. Such creatures are an innovation of the twentieth century. Once a part of the services, it is expected that entertainment items of all kinds must be included in the programme. For the pastor to tell "Aunt Sally" that her voice is not what it used to be, or to begin to cast out all the golden calves of entertainment requires more courage than Aaron had and certainly as much as filled the soul of Elijah.

The deleterious effect of entertainment in worship has to be reckoned with. The whole tone of the service is lowered. Seriousness and determination to grapple with the profundities of revelation decline. The minister's own standards in preaching deteriorate. He is flattered by his flock for his brevity, his anecdotes and his simplicity, yet placed alongside an expositor of power and incessant discipline the poor fellow is seen to have become a child, having lost any ability there might have been for detailed and authoritative preaching. Too many pastors' lives consist of running around keeping people happy and organising activities with less and less time spent in the exacting disciplines of the study. The result is that generalities are presented—a few little hastily plucked flowers amidst a spray of leaves which are all the same and which we have all seen before.

When a congregation becomes accustomed to a light diet of entertainment, and preaching which does not convict and reform there is great reluctance, and even antipathy, to change.

Naturally, pastors are reluctant to introduce reformation when traditional practices are entrenched. Time and wisdom are essential. Much teaching is needed but when willingness to conform to Scripture takes place then the Word of God prevails. When God-ordained men are recognised and their gifts developed and utilised in full measure according to Scripture, then we can say that the Word of God prevails *mightily*.

Because Paul did not summon the deacons to Miletus we must not think they are unimportant. The first deacons were appointed to relieve the apostles of practical work. This had so mounted in volume that the apostles were being hindered in their main task of prayer, teaching and oversight. Only seven deacons were chosen out of the thousands of church members, but they were almost certainly full-time (Acts 6: 1-6).

They were filled with the Holy Spirit and wisdom which was essential for their exacting work of discerning the needs of those requiring pecuniary help. Immediately following this description of the appointment of deacons we read, "And the Word of God increased and the number of disciples multiplied in Jerusalem greatly" (Acts 6: 7). The apostles were enabled to devote themselves wholly to their ministry of promulgating the word of life and the Lord was pleased to give continued increase to the church at Jerusalem.

We might summarise some of the blessings that follow when the Word of God prevails mightily in church order. 1. All members of the flock receive nurture not only by way of public teaching but by way of pastoral care from the elders. Thus all are built up and the potential of each member is developed, not only inwardly but by way of service. 2. Because of the support given them, the teaching elders are able to do justice to the Word of God as workers that need not to be ashamed, rightly dividing the word of truth. Thus the whole flock is instructed and the church established as "the pillar and ground of the truth" (1 Tim. 3: 15). 3. The elders and deacons are enabled to organise and attend to outreach whereby every household is visited throughout the area. 4. As the church grows in numbers and quality, attention can be given to missionary projects for the furtherance of the Gospel in unevangelised areas. 5. Those with suitable gifts can be set apart for particular or specialised areas of service either at home or abroad. Such specialisation obviously requires a stable and competent eldership to provide leadership and support.

4. The Word of God must prevail in daily life

The revival at Ephesus is described as the prevailing of God's Word in a mighty way. The results included the public burning of bad books, worth fifty thousand pieces of silver. Furthermore, such was the falling away of sales for images of Diana, that the whole city became involved in a riot (Acts 19: 26-41). These features are singled out by Luke as noteworthy indications of the reformation which took place in the Ephesian society. In fact, both the book-burning and the riot are negative and point to the removal and destruction of ungodliness.

Abundant life came in to replace the life of sin. Such life is in Christ alone (John 10: 10) and this life is imparted to believers as they heed all parts of Scripture. The Word prevails when all sin is forsaken and when a man is transformed through the renewing of his mind. No area of life is excluded from this transformation.

In defining revival we cannot exclude the idea of transformation or reformation. A true revival will result in renewal which begins in the church but which affects the whole fabric of society, as Christians wield their influence in that society. Ephesus is an example of this.

Francis Schaeffer in his writings has shown that we are moving rapidly into a post-Christian era. The moral values which we have inherited and which were established by the Reformation are disappearing, and a generation wholly under the influence of secular, humanistic, evolutionary philosophy is emerging.

In a feverish quest for remedies, Christians have put their trust in a variety of movements. The Jesus Revolution is an example. Some have thought in terms of Christian unity; others in terms of mass evangelism. Yet others, including many Baptists, have put their hope in a new charismatic movement. They think that if only the extraordinary gifts of the Spirit were recovered—tongues-speaking, miracles, healing and the like—this would lead to the renewal of the Christian church. Claims have been made that such a revival of the extraordinary gifts is taking place in several denominations. Some well-known Baptist ministers have wholeheartedly identified themselves with this quest for the extraordinary gifts. There have been "tarrying" meetings and reports have been circulated of believers being baptised in the Spirit and speaking with tongues.

With this news have come disquieting reports. Mature Christians have been disturbed by the fanaticism and immaturity of some involved. They have observed that obsession to recover the gifts has led to much that is discreditable. Rolling on the floor or shrieking slogans with hands outstretched has not commended itself to observers. It is not the Word of God, Jesus Christ and holy living that is the source of enthusiasm, but rather "experiences" *per se*. It is the experience that is boasted of, and the fruit by way of claims to greater love for Christ is added on to endorse the experience.

Having personally gone through some of these "experiences" in the pursuit of pentecostal gifts, I believe that the present movement is a mirage and a delusion and that to put one's trust in it is to lean upon a broken reed. Satan ever seeks to distract the people of God and lead them away from the genuine source of their health. The Holy Spirit exalts Christ and would have us concentrate upon sanctification by the Word of truth (John 17: 17; 2 Thess. 2: 13). I believe with all my heart that the teaching of Scripture as a whole indicates that the extraordinary era of the apostles, with the supernatural gifts then bestowed, was for the purpose of establishing all that we need by way of a foundation for the church. That foundation is represented in the completed Scriptures, which are all sufficient in the hands of the Spirit to meet every need of Christ's church until the end of time. Some seem to think that questions of this kind can be settled with a proof text or two but only through a thorough examination of passages such as Hebrews 2: 3, 4 can valid conclusions be reached. The charismatic movement fails to come to grips with the truly momentous issues of biblical theology, the peculiarities of the apostolic era, the development of revelation and the different dispensations in the history of redemption.

Truth is established from whole passages of Scripture and by careful comparison of one part with another. For instance, Paul in his address to the Ephesian elders makes no reference to miracles. His whole appeal there is to the example of his life and the same applies in his letters to the Thessalonians. The subject has been dealt with in detail elsewhere and many books have been devoted to this theme.[10] Enough here to assert that the way ahead, in my opinion, does not lie in a vain quest to recover what it is not the will of God to give, but rather our full concentration should be upon the Scriptures as a whole; doctrine, experience and practice. R. L. Dabney, the Southern Presbyterian theologian who had personal experience of revivals, said, "God who is never wasteful in his expedients (supernatural signs) withdrew them. Henceforward the church was to conquer the unbelief of the world by its example and teaching alone, energised by the illumination of the Holy Spirit."[11]

It is always fatal to exalt one area at the expense of another. Some of the Anabaptists at the time of the Reformation concentrated on ecstasies and visions and bordered upon madness. On the other hand to exalt doctrine alone will lead to barrenness. In Australia they nickname intellectual Calvinists "Dutchies"! A Dooyeweerdian branch of Dutch

Calvinism has seized some and made them unbalanced and the origin of the nickname may well be traced to this. Happily very few can grasp what the "Dutchies" are driving at and so the sect is restricted in size! Other forms of Calvinism sometimes harm what is known as the Reformed movement. Some are pessimistic in the extreme, are hyper-critical and never enquire after the progress of local churches. In short they are "wet blankets", and lack what the Ethiopian eunuch had when he went on his way. No wonder some become disillusioned with such a lifeless approach and "get sold" on seeking a new charismatic movement!

In contrast to unbalanced expressions of the Gospel it would be wonderful to see a great renewal of application of the Word of God in the homes of believers—husbands, wives and children serving the Lord with joy. A revival which embraces all aspects, including devoted faithfulness to church responsibilities and encouraging fellow believers to love and good works (Heb. 10: 24) is the crying need. To do all things well, to have knowledge and wisdom with regard to the different spheres of Christ's rule: civil government, family life and church life, this is real revival and reformation, and can come only through the outpouring of the Spirit upon the preaching of the Word.

There is no easy formula for the way ahead. The only way is for the Word of God to prevail, not one part of it, but the whole of it, and that mightily, to the quickening of God's people, and the salvation of our world which is hurtling to destruction.

To seek this is to seek something similar to the sixteenth-century Reformation. But there is a difference now. Society then was subject to Popery. Society now is mostly humanistic and secular. As pointed out in the first chapter, the Reformers fell short in their doctrine of the church. Their reformation awaits completion. We admire their great exploits. We are thankful for what they achieved. Observing the place they gave to Scripture let us go forward in the name of Christ. The opportunities are immense. The promises of God are immense. The way ahead is to labour night and day that the Word may prevail and that mightily. Let others rave about their idols, their notions, their schemes, their movements or themselves. Let our enthusiasm and zeal be for the whole of Scripture, and for the honour, glory and praise of our majestic Saviour and sovereign King.

REFERENCES

[1] The "Broadman Bible Commentary" is in the process of production. G. Henton Davies wrote Genesis and Roy L. Honeycut, Exodus. Davies is Principal of Regents Park College in Oxford.

[2] The motion was adopted by a vote of 5,394 to 2,170. The authors agreed to rewrite their material.

[3] *Christianity Today*, June 23, 1972. At the 1972 Convention a Dr. Hobbs spoke for retention of the Broadman commentary and for the liberal standpoint. He opposed the motion to withdraw the modernist Broadman commentary for five

reasons, and I quote from the tape: "1. I have never read a commentary with which I have fully agreed. 2. No man alive could write a commentary on the Bible with which all Southern Baptists would agree entirely [much applause]. 3. From the tape the third point is a jumble of casuistry but it adds up to the fact that no book must be regarded as a creed [applause]. 4. We must never take action against the competency of the soul in religion. 5. For three years we have wrestled with this subject and we need to put the matter behind us [applause]." If this is the kind of reasoning that prevailed to win the majority we can see the writing on the wall, "Thou art weighed in the balances and found wanting."

⁴ Copies are at present available from Carey Publications. *The Pastor's Dilemma*, 96 pp. 50p.

⁵ Arminius, from which name Arminianism is derived, was a Dutchman who lived in the seventeenth century. He denied the doctrine of election, of total depravity, of irresistible grace, of particular redemption and of the perseverance of the saints as taught by Calvin.

⁶ Peter Masters, minister of Spurgeon's Tabernacle, London, has written a twenty-four page booklet, *The Marks of Grace*, which analyses the Campus Crusade method. One of the finest studies available concerning short-cut methods is *Today's Gospel, Authentic or Synthetic?*, by Walter Chantry. 90 pp. Banner of Truth Trust.

⁷ *The Soul Winner.* Eerdmans, p. 96.

⁸ Never have we had more congresses on evangelism. These affairs seem organised to boost the work of evangelistic organisations. Their value is minimal. Evangelism is to be practised, not talked about, and very often those who debate about it most practise it the least.

⁹ The centrality of Ecumenism as a subject is illustrated by the fact that the Westminster Fraternal for ministers led by Dr. Martyn Lloyd-Jones insists that all who attend must be clear on this subject, and be against false ecumenicity.

¹⁰ *A Theology of the Holy Spirit*, by F. D. Bruner. Hodder. 390 pp. Is probably the most thorough treatment yet published. Classic works on the subject of the Holy Spirit and the gifts include John Owen's Works, Vols. 3 and 4, Jonathan Edwards' *Charity and its Fruits*, and *The Doctrine of the Holy Spirit*, by George Smeaton, all published by the Banner of Truth Trust. *What About Tongues Speaking*, Paternoster, 160 pp., is one of the best short books on the subject. John Stott, Eric Gurr, John Skilton and Stephen Short, have all written useful booklets, while R. G. Gromacki, D. W. Burdick and J. H. Pickford are Baptists in America who have written books on the subject.

¹¹ *Discussions: Evangelical and Theological.* Banner of Truth Trust. Vol. 2, p. 237.

AN ANABAPTIST
BIBLIOGRAPHY

THE standard volumes by G. H. Williams and L. Verduin referred to in the first chapter (p. 13) are at present out of print. Nevertheless, a comprehensive range of books is available. Alan Kreider of the London Mennonite Centre, 14 Shepherds Hill, Highgate, London N6 5AQ has kindly compiled the following bibliography. An excellent work of historical research has been achieved by those of Mennonite conviction on the subject of the Anabaptists. Many of the titles quoted are also available from the Christian Bookshop, 12 Forest Road, Edinburgh.

The best brief introduction to Anabaptism is provided by Harold S. Bender's 1943 presidential address to the American Society of Church History, which has been reprinted in pamphlet form as *The Anabaptist Vision*.[1] (This has also been reprinted in a collection of essays in Bender's honour edited by G. F. Hershberger entitled *The Recovery of the Anabaptist Vision*.)[1] More recently, three lengthier popular introductions to Anabaptist history and thought have appeared. *The Anabaptist Story*[1] by the American Baptist church historian W. R. Estep (Eerdmans: 1975) is the most extensive of these, and combines a narrative of Anabaptist history with chapters which analyse the cardinal tenets of the movement. Cornelius J. Dyck has edited *An Introduction to Mennonite History*[1] (Herald: 1967) which draws on the learning of many leading Mennonite scholars. In addition to its treatment of subsequent Mennonite history, the first 111 pages provide a concise study of the early Anabaptists. In the third volume, Walter Klaassen's *Anabaptism: Neither Catholic nor Protestant*[2] (Conrad: 1973), presents an interesting, and at times controversial, study of Anabaptist thought; he includes very little narrative.

In recent years, a number of important specialist studies in English have also appeared. Two of these are quite broad in scope though scholarly in character. Robert Friedmann's *The Theology of Anabaptism*[1] (Herald: 1973) is significantly subtitled *An Interpretation*. Although full of sympathy and penetrating remarks, it is less systematic and exhaustive than its title would imply. More successful as a work of scholarship is

Claus-Peter Clasen's *Anabaptism: A Social History* (London: Cornell U.P.: 1972), which presents a superbly researched study of Central European Anabaptism full of fascinating information. The author is as unfriendly to the Anabaptists as Friedmann is emphatic; and some of his judgments do go awry. However, this is a very significant work from which all will learn.

Recent monographs on specific tenets of Anabaptist belief include R. S. Armour's *Anabaptist Baptism*[1] (Herald: 1966), which was awarded the American Society of Church History's highest award; Franklin H. Littell's *The Origins of Sectarian Protestantism*[1] (originally published in 1952 as *The Anabaptist View of the Church*); and James M. Stayer's, *Anabaptists and the Sword*[2] (Coronado: 1972).

Among regional studies are John S. Oyer's illuminating study of Central German Anabaptism and the Reformers (*Lutheran Reformers against Anabaptists* [Nijhoff: 1964]); Cornelius Krahn's *Dutch Anabaptism*[1] (Nijhoff: 1968); A. L. E. Verheyden's *Anabaptism in Flanders*[1] (Herald: 1961); and most interesting for readers in this country, I. B. Horst's *The Radical Brethren: Anabaptism and the English Reformation to 1558*[2] (De Graaf, 1972).

Although the *Täuferaktenkommission* continues to make progress in the publication of Anabaptist documents in the original languages, the number of available sources in English remains all too small. Unfortunately G. H. Williams's edition of selected Anabaptist writings in the Library of Christian Classics is out of print. Nevertheless, a number of essential Anabaptist texts are available. Primary among these is the monumental volume of *The Complete Writings of Menno Simons*[1] (Herald: 1956) in the edition of Leonard Verduin and J. C. Wenger. Crucially important early texts are Conrad Grebel's *Programmatic Letters of 1524*[1] (Herald: 1970), available in facsimile in an edition by J. C. Wenger; and the writings of the man who in many ways was the most important of the early Anabaptists, Michael Sattler (John H. Yoder, ed., *The Legacy of Michael Sattler*[1] (Herald: 1973). The latter contains the famous Schleitheim Confession. The best-known writing of Hutterite Anabaptism, and in many ways the most topically organised document produced by a sixteenth-century Anabaptist, is Peter Rideman's *Confession of Faith*. This work, which Rideman wrote in the enforced leisure of prison life, is available from Plough Publishing Company (Darvell, Robertsbridge, East Sussex TN32 5DR). The graphically-written and often deeply moving martyrology of Thielemann J. van Braght, *The Bloody Theater or Martyrs Mirror of the Defenseless Christians who Baptised only upon Confession of Faith*,[1] has been for Mennonite believers what John Foxe's *Acts and Monuments* was for the English Puritans; its most recent edition is Herald: 1949.

[1] Available if ordered from Highgate.

[2] Can be obtained by special order.

REFLECTIONS ON THE LORD'S SUPPER

These comments are made with special reference to the chart on pages 40 and 41.

In the chart depicting English Baptist History there is a note testifying to the fact that most Particular Baptists have adhered in their practice to Strict Communion. This means that only those who have been baptised by immersion have been regarded as eligible and been invited to the Lord's table. For instance, J. H. Oncken held to this view and advocated it for all the churches he was instrumental in planting.

There are degrees in the application of Strict Communion. Some restrict participation to those who belong to the same denomination—'same faith and order', as is practised by the Gospel Standard Baptists (see chart). The more common practice is to restrict communion to baptised (by immersion) believers only.

In our day when discipline is frowned upon as an enemy of free expression and human liberty, this restriction of the Lord's table to baptised believers is regarded as narrow-minded. The cry goes up that it is *the Lord's table*, not a table to be restricted by man. Yet the apostle Paul warned strongly about the dangers of careless communion and the peril of eating and drinking damnation to oneself. This would seem to imply care. Careless people will not of themselves be careful. If there is to be any discipline it will come from those appointed by Christ to oversee his flock and his ordinances; to protect the lambs and keep out the wolves. If Christ exhorted that ordinary believers exercise discernment in this matter how much more the elders of the churches?

The main passage upon which strict communion is upheld is Acts 2: 38-42 which describes the church order adhered to throughout the New Testament. This order was never broken. At least we have no record of it ever being broken. What is the order? The answer is, repentance toward God, faith in the Lord Jesus Christ, baptism by immersion, followed by membership with the body of Christ in the local church. Immersion baptism is primarily the symbol of total union with Christ in his death, burial and resurrection. That union is not only with Christ the head, it is with the Church which is his body. Faithful church membership is seen in the steadfast continuance in the apostles' doctrine and fellowship, breaking of bread and prayers.

124

All the converts without exception followed this order in New Testament times. It was not a case of someone contradicting Peter or the apostles by saying, "Well I don't agree when you say, 'Be immersed every one of you!' I refuse to do that and will go straight to the table. Let others be baptised but not me!" When Paul went to Ephesus, even though the twelve men with whom he met had been immersed with John's baptism, Paul insisted on a Christian immersion. To Paul, Christian baptism was not optional. The early Christians took Christ's commands seriously. They did not play fast and loose with them. Christ has not commanded that we keep the complicated rituals of the Levitical order. He has simply commanded that they who believe be baptised and that they should commemorate his atonement with a supper of bread and wine.

When it comes to practice today, we apply precisely the same order as applied in apostolic times. We maintain that this is required by the New Testament. As our converts are instructed and prepared for immersion we will not allow that others who have never submitted to and obeyed this command pass ahead of them to the table. That would be to maintain double standards. In local Baptist churches, therefore, only those who obey Christ's command can be members and only those who obey can sit down to the table.

There is one way in which this can be unjust, that is in the case of visitors who are sincere, practising believers from non-Baptist churches. Are they to be turned away? Some Baptist churches simply require that any visitor make his desire known to one of the elders before he communes. Providing he is a member in good standing with a Bible-believing, evangelical church, then he may commune. If, however, he is under discipline or censure in another church, or a wanderer evading the responsibilities of church membership, he definitely may not sit down. The communion table is not a "free-for-all", it is a communion of those united in Christ. Union with Christ is a serious matter requiring a consistent obedience and practice. Should the visitor find employment in the area and settle down then he must, if he wishes to be a member of a Baptist church, submit to the order of that church. If he is not willing to do this then it is better to be joined to another church. Any church (the word church means "called-out ones") worth its salt will have its own disciplinary requirements.

Whatever criticism may be levelled at Baptists for the discipline they maintain, let it be clearly understood that they will, if faithful, follow what they see to be the New Testament order. This results in united churches of serious Christian people of one mind. Churches with this New Testament order are structured to endure for centuries and happy examples can be cited of this. Neither for the rewards, nor for prosperity, but because we see that Christ requires it, do the main body of Baptists, unashamedly and boldly follow strict communion. It is Christ's table. Precisely because it is his table he has made provision that it be regulated with order and justice. "If ye love me," he said, "keep my commandments."

INDEX